The Golden Age of
Children's Television

Geoff Tibballs

TITAN BOOKS

Also available from Titan Books:

Film/TV tie-ins

Clive Barker's The Nightbreed Chronicles
Darkman
Dr Who Script Books 1-4
Don't Panic: The Hitch-hiker's Guide to
the Galaxy Companion
The Gerry Anderson Episode Guide
Gerry Anderson paperbacks:
Captain Scarlet and Thunderbirds 1 & 2
Giger's Alien
The Making of Dick Tracy
The Making of Terminator 2
The Official Batman Batbook
Ray Harryhausen's Film Fantasy Scrapbook

Star Trek publications

Captain's Log
The Making of Star Trek
Mr Scott's Guide to the Enterprise
Star Fleet Technical Manual
The Star Trek Compendium
The Star Trek Interview Book
Star Trek novels 1-52
Star Trek giant novels 1-6
Star Trek: The Next Generation novels 1-19
Star Trek: The Next Generation giant novels 1 & 2
The Worlds of the Federation

The Golden Age of Children's Television

ISBN 1 85286 407 9

Published by Titan Books Ltd,
19 Valentine Place, London SE1 8QH

First edition November 1991
10 9 8 7 6 5 4 3 2 1

Specialised research consultant: Henry Scott-Irvine.

Printed and bound in England by Hillman Printers (Frome) Ltd,
Frome, Somerset.

A CIP record for this publication is available from the
British Library.

Contents

Dedicated to the memory of the late
Harry Corbett.

Acknowledgements:

The author would like to express his thanks to the following for kindly digging deep into their memories and filing cabinets to provide anecdotes and photographs:

Kathryn de Belle at Granada Television, British Film Institute, Sean Burke, Channel 4, Matthew Corbett, M. Georges Croses, Leslie Crowther, Jan Dalibor, Ellipse, David Ellison, Frank Fehmers Productions, FilmFair, Peter Firmin and Oliver Postgate at Smallfilms, Bob Godfrey Films, Terry Hall, Hanna-Barbera, Hilary Hayton, Pip Hinton, Bob Holness, Brian Jeeves at Yorkshire Television, Jon Keeble at ITC, King Rollo Films, Hilary Kingsley, Peter Lane, Nick Lockett at Central Television, London Weekend Television, Rowena Mafham, Desi Maxim at Thames Television, Christine McClair at British Sky Broadcasting, Bobbie Mitchell at BBC Picture Archives, Johnny Morris, M. Gerard Neuvecelle, Roy North, Primetime, John Ryan, Claire Silverman at the BBC, Television South-West, Christopher Trace, Bert Weedon, Westbourne Films, Wally Whyton, Leila Williams, Muriel Young.

Thanks also to everyone at Titan Books for their unbounded enthusiasm about everything from *Wacky Races* to *Camberwick Green*, to my wife Carol for compiling the index and for not marrying David Hedison from *Voyage to the Bottom of the Sea*, and to my daughters Nicola and Lindsey for lending me their *Pinky and Perky* video. Some day I'll let them have it back.

Foreword

The golden age

Above *Johnny Morris in* The Hot Chestnut Man.

We didn't know what we were really doing. Like kids in a classroom, we had been given a lump of plasticine and told to make something out of it. What? Don't ask daft questions, go and do it. Draw on your experience, your memories and your imagination: you call yourself an entertainer, go on then, entertain us. That, roughly, was what we were told. We didn't realise how lucky we were. The Golden Age of Children's Television matured largely because we were left alone. There were no theorists around for no one knew what to theorise about. The people in charge merely steered us gently along: "Left hand down a bit, not too much, now right hand, that's better." They let us be us. They assumed the attitude of reasonably intelligent, sensitive onlookers. This was very wise of them, for most of the things that were happening on television were happening for the first time. It was all original since there was nothing from which to copy, and so most suggestions were readily accepted. I had the idea of dressing up as a zoo keeper, going in with the animals and making them talk. They said, "Yes, go and do it." It was a golden opportunity. I doubt if it would get past the planners today. It could be that only golden opportunities produce Golden Ages.

Johnny Morris, Bristol, 1991.

1950
- Birth of *Watch With Mother* on BBC. Its first star is *Andy Pandy*.
- Richard Hearne creates Mr Pastry.

1952
- *The Flowerpot Men* is added to *Watch With Mother*.
- Gerald Campion begins life as *Billy Bunter of Greyfriars School*.
- Sooty makes his TV debut.

1953
- *Rag, Tag and Bobtail* joins *Watch With Mother*.

1954
- Michael Bentine introduces *The Bumblies*.
- *The Cisco Kid* hits town.

1955
- *Picture Book* and *The Woodentops* complete the *Watch With Mother* line-up.
- Eamonn Andrews presents the first *Crackerjack*.
- ITV marks its arrival with *The Adventures of Robin Hood*.
- Death of Annette Mills, creator of Muffin the Mule.

1956
- New series include *The Adventures of Sir Lancelot*, *The Buccaneers*, *Lassie*, *The Lone Ranger*, *Champion the Wonder Horse*, *The Adventures of Superman* and *Zoo Time*.
- Lenny the Lion makes his bow.

1957
- The Toddlers' Truce is abolished. Now programmes can be shown between 6pm and 7pm.
- Debuts of Pinky and Perky, *Fury* and *Captain Pugwash*.

1958
- Christopher Trace and Leila Williams introduce the first *Blue Peter*.
- Among new ITV heroes are *Ivanhoe* and *William Tell*.

1959
- Pussy Cat Willum joins *Small Time*.
- Huckleberry Hound and his gang first appear on British TV.

1960
- Debuts of *Tales of the Riverbank*, *Ivor the Engine* and *The Sagas of Noggin the Nog*.

1961
- *Supercar* marks Gerry Anderson's first venture into sci-fi.
- Britain welcomes *The Flintstones*.

1962
- Start of *Animal Magic*, *Top of the Form* and *Tingha and Tucker*.

The Golden Years

1963
- William Hartnell becomes the first *Dr Who*.
- The Andersons create *Fireball XL5*.
- New cartoon characters are Top Cat and Deputy Dawg.

1964
- Birth of *Vision On*, *Play School* and *Pogle's Wood*.
- The Seaview begins its *Voyage to the Bottom of the Sea* and *Stingray* is launched.

1965
- Time for *The Magic Roundabout*.
- *Thunderbirds* is the latest from Gerry and Sylvia Anderson.
- *Jackanory* offers a new look to story-time.
- Debut of *Lost in Space*.

1966
- *The Monkees* takes Britain by storm.
- So does *Batman* and, in a more restrained manner, *Camberwick Green*.

1967
- The arrival of colour television.
- Gerry Anderson produces *Captain Scarlet and the Mysterons*.
- The *Trumpton* fire brigade answer their first 999.

1968
- Basil Brush begins his own show on BBC.
- Sooty and Pinky and Perky defect to ITV.

- New series include *Magpie*, *Joe 90*, *Land of the Giants* and *Hector's House*.

1969
- *Star Trek* first shown in the UK along with *Wacky Races* and *The Clangers*.
- Colour comes to BBC 1 and ITV.

1970
- *Catweazle* leaps forward in time.
- ITV introduces *Ace of Wands* and *Timeslip*.

1972
- First edition of *Rainbow*.
- Other newcomers include *The Adventures of Black Beauty*, *Clapperboard* and *Arthur of the Britons*.

1973
- Premiere of *The Wombles* and *The Tomorrow People*.

1974
- *Bagpuss* comes to life.

1975
- Jimmy Savile Fixes It for the first time.
- Chris Tarrant, Lenny Henry and Sally James host the new network Saturday morning show, *Tiswas*.

"Andy is waving goodbye"

In the beginning was Muffin the Mule. And he begat Andy Pandy who in turn begat The Flowerpot Men and Rag, Tag and Bobtail. Then, lo, one day a huge Spotty Dog came amongst them. And the children of the kingdom did rejoice.

In those far-off post-war days when rationing was rife and Cliff Richard really was a Young One, children had to make their own entertainment. Legend has it that hours of unbridled fun could be had with a stick and a top and a bag of marbles. Raffia ruled, OK. There was no Lego, no aliens to zap on Space Invaders, not even any Australian soap operas. Indeed, television was still in nappies. Not only was it geographically restricted to certain areas of Britain and, because of the price of sets, available merely to the privileged, but just one hour of the week was devoted to children's programmes — on a Sunday teatime.

In 1950 less than one home in twenty owned a television, but this was to be a key year in the development of children's programmes. Without the events of 1950, we may never have been able to covet a *Crackerjack* pencil, marvel at the sheer bravery of the *Trumpton* fire brigade or learn how to make a fully operational surface-to-air missile out of sticky-backed plastic, detergent bottles and one of Val's old bra straps.

For 1950 was the year that children's television came of age. The BBC increased its children's output to three days a week (Wednesday and Friday were added to Sunday) and introduced its trailblazing new series for the very young, *Watch With Mother*. The first star of *Watch With Mother* was a gent in a natty blue and white pinstriped suit with matching headgear. His name was Andy Pandy.

But before discussing the vagaries of Andy's wardrobe, a word about the guy who at the time was the undisputed king of kiddies' TV — **Muffin the Mule**.

Below *Annette Mills gets it straight from the horse's mouth - well, Muffin's - in* Muffin the Mule.

Left *Time to go home for Looby Loo, Andy Pandy and Teddy - in* Watch with Mother.

"Here comes Muffin, Muffin the Mule,
Dear old Muffin, playing the fool"
was the first signature tune to catch on. It also has the distinction of being one of the few old favourites not subsequently covered by Sinitta.

Muffin had been bought by puppeteer Ann Hogarth for 15s 0d from a travelling showman and was rescued from the anonymity of a workshop shelf by Annette Mills, sister of actor John

Louise the lamb, Sally the sea-lion, and **Prudence and Primrose Kitten** who were rewarded with their own spin-off shows.

But life was not so kind to Annette Mills. Her original ambition was to be a dancer, but she fell and broke a leg while dancing and had to sit out that career. Then, during the war she was involved in a car smash in the middle of an air raid and spent three years in hospital. Her

Above *Annette Mills with those fifties puppet favourites, Prudence and Primrose Kitten.*

Mills. She included the wooden mule in an edition of *For the Children* in 1946, along with a clown called Crumpet. Alas, Crumpet didn't have that certain screen charisma and was hastily dropped from the act and consigned to obscurity to become a Pete Best-like figure.

Meanwhile, Muffin went from strength to strength, clumping around limbs-a-kimbo on the piano top with Annette Mills playing the music and Ann Hogarth standing on the piano to operate him from behind a partition. After Crumpet's demise further sidekicks emerged, including a bossy penguin called Mr Peregrine,

first visit to the BBC to give a radio talk was actually made on crutches. She died in 1955, aged sixty-one, following an operation. It was the end of Muffin's fame too.

Watch With Mother was the brainchild of the legendary Freda Lingstrom, a formidable lady who became Head of Children's Television at the BBC. Together with Mary Adams, then the Corporation's Head of Television Talks, Miss Lingstrom created **Andy Pandy**.

With that pallid face reminiscent of an early David Bowie and dressed in the world's first shell suit, Andy started out as a solo act before being joined by his two pals, a doll named Looby Loo and a somewhat moth-eaten Teddy. Maria Bird brought Andy out to play, opera singer Gladys Whitred sang the songs and Audrey Atterbury and Molly Gibson pulled the strings. And what strings they were — thick enough to support a tent.

Andy and co lived in a large basket, to which they returned after each adventure. Heaven knows what they got up to in there all week, but in those days there seemed nothing irregular about two boys and a girl in a basket *a trois*.

Only twenty-six shows were made but they were repeated over a period of twenty years. And they all ended with the familiar song:

"Time to go home, time to go home.
Andy is waving goodbye, goodbye."

Two years later, in 1952, the same team brought us those two likely lads, **The Flowerpot Men**. Bill and Ben were the Bros of their day — except that arguably their lyrics were better than those of the Goss twins. It was almost impossible to tell The Flowerpot Men apart, although I reckon Bill's voice used to be an octave higher. Perhaps he'd had a nasty experience with a garden fork. Those wonderful "flibadobs" and "flobadobs", which some parents claimed were impairing their offspring's speech development, were the work of Peter Hawkins, the man who later put words into the mouths of Captain Pugwash and the Daleks.

Bill and Ben's

escapades took place behind the potting shed in a plot of land owned by a sinister but unseen gardener. The merest hint of the approach of THE GARDENER was enough to send Bill and Ben scurrying down into their pots.

The burning issue of the day was always: "Was it Bill or was it Ben?", a *Columbo*-style mystery able to be solved by only one being — the Little Weed that stood between the two flowerpots. Down the years eminent historians have pondered on the significance of Little Weed. How come she knew everything? Was "Ipple Weeb", as she was known, an agent for

Below Bill tells Ben how he came within an inch of being Britain's first kebab - in The Flowerpot Men.

the Eastern Bloc? Was she somehow connected with Burgess and Maclean? Or was she just a plant? Was there a mole? And if so, why didn't the gardener do something about it?

The next addition to *Watch With Mother*, in 1953, was **Rag, Tag and Bobtail**, Louise Cochrane's delightful stories about a hedgehog, a mouse and a rabbit, told by Charles E. Stidwell. At the time I thought they were the cutest little creatures imaginable, although with hindsight it has to be said that they do look more like vermin. They went out on Thursday, following *Andy Pandy* (Tuesday) and *The Flowerpot Men* (Wednesday). The famous five were completed in 1955 with the arrival of *Picture Book* (Monday) and *The Woodentops* (Friday).

The principal storyteller on **Picture Book** was Patricia Driscoll, who went on to make the men merrie as Maid Marian in *The Adventures of Robin Hood*. Since *Picture Book* was prere-

__Above__ Patricia Driscoll's successor on the programme Picture Book*, Vera McKechnie.*
__Right__ Daddy Woodentop never bit his nails – because they were holding his shoulders in place.

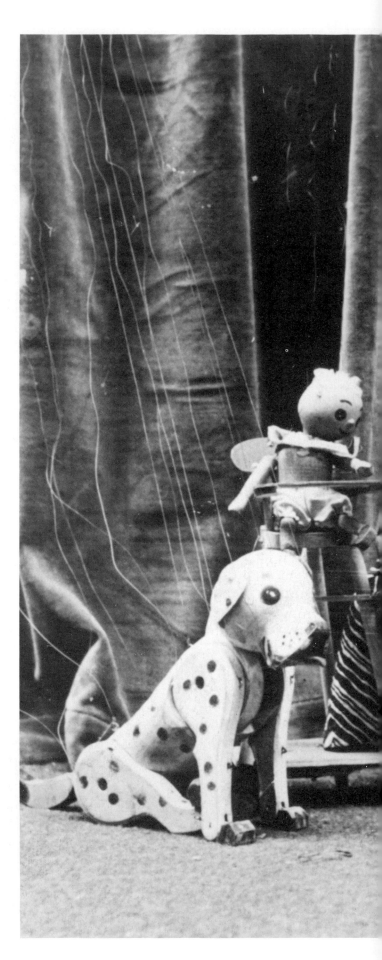

corded in bits and pieces and the BBC had no idea how the sections would fit together, Patricia had to wear the same dress, or an identical copy, for nigh on a year. She says: "I used to get letters from people pitying me, saying, 'Please could we buy you another dress as you've obviously only got the one?'"

The Woodentops comprised Mummy and Daddy Woodentop, the twins Willy and Jenny, baby Woodentop, Mrs Scrubbitt the daily help (very middle class the Woodentops), Sam the farmhand, Buttercup the cow and the star of the show, "the biggest spotty dog you ever did see." Spotty was famed for his weird bark and mechanical movements and perfected a silly walk when John Cleese was barely out of short trousers.

Watch With Mother established the weekday early afternoon slot as a haven for toddlers safe from the corruptive physical exhibitionism of *Come Dancing*, the head-banging sounds of

CHIGLEY CHARACTERS

Lord Belborough
Mr Brackett the butler
Mr Cresswell the biscuit factory manager
Mr Clamp the greengrocer
Thomas Tripp the milkman
Willie Munn
Mr Rumpling the bargee
Mr Farthing
Mr Swallow
farmer Jonathan Bell
Roger Varley the chimney sweep
PC McGarry
Mr Crockett the garage owner
Dr Mopp

Below Mr Cresswell shows Lord Belborough and Mr Brackett the biscuit factory at Chigley, Trumptonshire.

"Andy is waving goodbye"

Eric Robinson's *Music For You* and the wanton violence of *Dixon of Dock Green*. It was subsequently occupied by all manner of favourites — **Barnaby**, **Chigley**, **The Herbs** (complete with Dill the dog, the Chives, Lady Rosemary, Sir Basil and, of course, Parsley the Lion, who graduated to his own spin-off series), **Bizzy Lizzy**, the bowler-hatted **Mr Benn** and his costume shop adventures, **Joe**, those clever little finger puppets **Fingerbobs** and the girl, dog and mouse caper, **Mary, Mungo and Midge**.

Left *Joe, the little boy whose dad ran a café near a lorry park. Lee Montague was the narrator.*
Above *Barnaby the bear admires Maisie Mole's handiwork.*
Below left *Mr Benn tried on a different costume each day. Happily he restricted himself to men's clothes.*
Below right *Flower power! To make her dreams come true, Bizzy Lizzy touched the wishing flower on her dress.*

Above The Herbs, with Parsley the lion, of course, occupying centre stage.
Right If you went down to the woods in the sixties, you could have bumped into The Pogles.

THE HERBS CHARACTERS

Parsley the lion
Dill the dog
Sage the owl
Constable Knapweed (PC 29)
Mr Bayleaf the gardener
Mr Onion
Sir Basil and Lady Rosemary
Aunt Mint
The Chives
Tarragon
Belladonna
Pashana Bedhi

From Smallfilms, the prolific stable of Oliver Postgate and Peter Firmin, came *The Pogles*, *The Clangers* and *Bagpuss*. One of the mainstays of **The Pogles** was a witch, but the BBC wasn't too keen on witches in children's programmes so the title changed to *Pogles' Wood* and the saucy sorceress was sent packing on her broomstick. Young viewers were left to enjoy the antics of a magic bean plant, Mr and Mrs Pogle, Pippin and Tog. **The Clangers** followed in 1969, the year man landed on the moon. They were described by a NASA scientist as "an attempt to bring a note of realism to the fantasy of the space race." Major Clanger and his family were small mouse-shaped creatures

WHY ARE THEY CALLED CLANGERS?

Well, that is not a difficult question. Their world does not have a thick overcoat of atmosphere like our world. So meteorites and odd bits of rock and even odder things that happen to be hurtling about in space often come down with a bump on the outside of the Clangers' planet. Because of this, the Clangers live inside their planet and wear armour plates. They go into their planet through holes which are protected with stout metal lids. It is the cling-clang-clonk sound which these lids make when they are slammed shut that gives the Clangers their name.

– *The Clangers Annual 1971*

Above Fat cat, Bagpuss cat.
Below Captain Flack of the Trumpton Fire Brigade on the hot line.

Above *The Mayor of Trumpton consults with Town Clerk Mr Troop before leaving to inspect the gas works.*

who lived on a blue moon and were surrounded by such delightful peripheral characters as the Soup Dragon, the Iron Chicken and the Froglets. **Bagpuss** was a fat, lazy, cloth cat who rested on a cushion in Emily's magic shop window and came to life to play with the toy mice on their mouse organ, Madeleine the doll, a banjo-playing toad called Gabriel and Professor Yaffle, a wooden woodpecker bookend. Only thirteen shows were made but they have been repeated by the BBC no fewer than twenty-seven times.

Forget *Compact* and *The Newcomers*, life was much more exciting in Gordon Murray's animated soap operas, **Camberwick Green** and **Trumpton**. The hero of *Camberwick Green* was Windy Miller, while many of the tales of *Trumpton* revolved around those intrepid fire-fighters Hugh, Pugh, Barney McGrew, Cuthbert, Dibble and Grubb.

Above Drama at Camberwick Green as Dr Mopp harangues milkman Thomas Tripp about the mess outside his house.

CAMBERWICK GREEN CHARACTERS

Peter the postman
Mrs Dingle the postmistress
Packet the post office puppy
Dr Mopp
Mrs Honeyman the chemist's wife
Mickey Murphy the baker
Mr Carraway the fishmonger
Windy Miller
Mr Crockett the garage owner
Thomas Tripp the milkman
Paddy & Mary Murphy
Roger Varley the chimney sweep
PC McGarry
Mr Dagenham the salesman
Captain Snort who ran Pippin Fort

And who could forget **Tales of the Riverbank**, the exploits of Hammy Hamster, Roderick the Rat and Mr Guinea Pig, known to his friends as 'G.P.' ? Filmed in Canada and sold to forty-eight countries, it is still being screened today in various corners of the world, making it the longest running filmed TV series.

It all looked so natural on screen, but creator/producer David Ellison reveals that the animals' actions were carefully choreographed: "They were actually directed in that the scenes were set up so that they could only take one route. The way they stopped and rubbed their noses was planned too. I used to lick my finger and then touch Hammy's nose with it. I would then place him on the set and gently blow on his nose. The cool air would react on the damp nose and Hammy would automatically stop and rub it. And if I was really lucky, he'd rub behind his ear too.

"To make them appear to talk, we would give them something to eat and then just film the last few munches. But hamsters, rats and guinea pigs are such fast twitchers that we had to slow the action down, otherwise Johnny Morris, who did the English narration, would never have been able to keep up."

But how did Hammy appear to be a better drummer than Ringo? Ellison explains: "We stuck the drumsticks to Hammy's hands with jam. A hamster's natural reaction to having jam on his paws is to try and shake it off, so for a few seconds it looked as if Hammy was drumming.

"It was the same with Roderick the Rat. He was supposed to be a concert pianist. We used to spread cream cheese on the music sheet and place his feet on the piano keys. As he sniffed the cheese, he got right up close to the music sheet as if he was a short-sighted pianist. And as he moved along the sheet in pursuit of the cheese, his feet would move along the keyboard to make it appear that he was playing the piano!"

But there were hitches. "The lighting in

those days was so intense," says Ellison, "that after only ten minutes' action, the animals would curl up in a ball and go to sleep. Also hamsters are only photogenic for nine months — they then go old and grey. In all, I reckon we got through 100 Hammys. When we finished with them, we gave them to friends and they were used for breeding. The world must be full of descendants of Hammy Hamster.

"The animals were never taken out of the studio though. Dummies were used for exterior shots. It was just as well because once we lost a hot air balloon and it sailed off over Ontario. Luckily its occupant was just a Madame Tussaud's version of Hammy."

That is indeed a merciful relief. I don't think I would be able to sleep at night for thinking that somewhere up there floating around in the skies was a real Hammy Hamster. ✳

Below Not a lot of people know that Hammy Hamster wrote all his own scripts for Tales of the Riverbank.

Chapter 2

"It's through the round window"

 or many future dustmen, sportsmen, tree surgeons or captains of industry, **Play School** was the first TV series they watched regularly. Everyone remembers different things about *Play School*. Some think of Big Ted, others the *Play School* house, or maybe Brian Cant's wit and energy or Derek Griffiths' miming ability. But to the fashion industry, it was the show which popularised the dungaree.

Prior to *Play School*, dungarees had mainly been worn by painters and decorators to absorb wayward splashes of emulsion in the brief periods between tea breaks. But when young mums saw right-on TV presenters wearing them, they suddenly realised the garment could be trendy as well as practical. Before long the school gates was the setting for a daily dungaree convention.

Play School was created by Joy Whitby in 1964 to cater for pre-school children in the two

***

SOME PLAY SCHOOL PRESENTERS

Chloe Ashcroft	Johnny Ball
Floella Benjamin	Stuart Bradley
Brian Cant	Carol Chell
Miranda Connell	Simon Davies
Derek Griffiths	Fred Harris
Wayne Jackman	Brian Jameson
Rick Jones	Iain Lauchlan
Carol Leader	Lionel Morton
Carmen Munroe	Johnny Silvo
Don Spencer	Julie Stevens
Eric Thompson	Carol Ward

***

to five age group on the new BBC2 channel (it later switched to BBC1). Featuring music, games, poems, stories and play ideas, it aimed to be informative as well as entertaining. It prepared tiny minds for school by using the correct vocabulary. There were no pussies, baa-lambs and bunny-wunnies here. They were always cats, lambs and rabbits.

Children (not to mention dads on shiftwork) sat on the edges of their seats waiting to discover which window of the *Play School* house they were going to look through today. The programme was by no means confined to the studio, often heading off for learning adventures at the zoo, the park or the seaside. Brian Cant was very much the show's mainstay, his boundless enthusiasm making him a sort of junior Stuart Hall.

Play School had the distinction of being the first children's TV programme to be preserved for posterity when in 1982 George Howard, then the BBC chairman, buried tapes of the show in a radiation proof capsule in the grounds of his stately home, Castle Howard in Yorkshire. It

Left Play School *presenters 1969 vintage - Rick Jones and Julie Stevens - with the toys.*

PLAY SCHOOL TOYS

Big Ted
Bingo (a knitted dog)
Cuckoo (a woolly bird)
Hamble
Humpty
Jemima the rag doll
Little Ted
Poppy (a black doll)

was all part of the BBC's sixtieth birthday party, the hope being that the capsule would not be opened until 3982, 2,000 years later. I wonder what our distant generations will make of dungarees.

As for a radiation proof capsule, we know a song about that, don't we?

For nearly twenty years, Britain's under-fives have been hooked on the antics of a big bear, a pink hippopotamus, an odd creature with a zip for a mouth and a refugee from *Z Cars*. The object of their affection is Thames Television's **Rainbow**, starring Bungle, George, Zippy and Geoffrey Hayes, formerly Detective Constable Scatliff at Newtown CID.

The first host back in 1972 was actor David Cook, who was joined by Moony, a meek mauve puppet, and Sunshine, an aggressive yellow one. But then today's favourites arrived, although for Geoffrey Hayes it required certain adjustments to his principles.

Back in the early seventies, Matthew Corbett, who now presents *Sooty*, was combining helping his late father Harry with the little bear's TV series and acting in repertory. While in rep at Dundee, Matthew met Geoffrey who was by then an established actor through his role in *Z Cars*. Matthew says: "For some reason Geoffrey didn't like me and we had a terrible row about my going off to do Sooty's Christmas Special. He ended up saying: 'That's not what acting's about. I just cannot believe how anybody can sell their soul and work with puppets and do such stupid things.' He was really vitriolic and we nearly came to blows, it was ever so close.

Above One that K-Tel missed out on.
Right Before handling Sooty, Matthew Corbett (centre) was part of Rainbow's Rod, Jane and Matthew.

"When two years later I got a job on *Rainbow*, I walked into the studio and who should I find but Geoffrey Hayes as the show's new presenter! Our eyes met. I knew that he knew that I remembered what had happened in Dundee and there he was standing with George, Zippy and Bungle, knowing that nobody else in the studio was aware of what he had said about it being a ridiculous way to earn a living. Nothing was said at the time and it's been an understanding ever since that whenever we meet, we don't mention it. I must emphasise, though, that we get along fine now."

Matthew's role on *Rainbow* was as one-third of the singing trio Rod, Jane and Matthew. And thereby hangs a tale. For Jane used to live with Rod but now lives with Matthew's successor, Freddy! Eat your heart out, *Dallas*.

In its early days *Rainbow* boasted some distinguished story-tellers, including Judi Dench and Stephanie Beacham. Remarkably for one who was to play superbitch Sable in *The Colbys*, Stephanie was in awe of appearing on *Rainbow* and decided to calm her nerves by practising story-telling in front of her own young children and their friends. But after an attentive couple of minutes, her audience walked out one by one in boredom. Even her own children left. Needless to say, the experience did little for Stephanie's confidence.

Other favourites of the very young included **The Adventures of Noddy** (one of ITV's first infant shows), the tales of **Buddy Bud-** gerigar with Peter Butterworth, **Rupert**, **Hatty Town** (a milliner's delight, where all the hats had personalities of their own), **Colonel Crock**, presented by Edward Andrews and featuring the adventures of vintage cars adorned in deerstalkers and monocles, and that impish boxer puppy **Bengo**, who was so cute you'd forgive him for running off with the last sheet of toilet roll. The escapades of Bengo were drawn by William Timyn, better known as 'Tim', and related by Sylvia Peters, the BBC's golden girl of the fifties. Bengo's ten minute stories were an integral part of the early *Blue Peter* programmes, along with those space age heroes **Bleep and Booster**.

Oliver Postgate and Peter Firmin first worked together on **Alexander the Mouse**, a

live series for ITV performed with magnetic animation. "The only problem with having characters operated by magnets underneath," recalls Postgate, "was that they were prone to suddenly turn upside down or, worse still, leap in the air and do a back somersault if approached incorrectly with the magnetic poles. When that hap-

Top Noddy tends his garden and then sweats while Mr Plod of the Toyland Sweeney checks his tax disc.
Above Rupert takes two dodgy hitch-hikers through Nut Wood and doesn't even take his scarf off for tea.

pened there was no alternative but to reach onto the set and stand the character up again. And since it was live, that almighty hand was seen on screen. All in all, I'm not so sorry that none of the shows exist today."

Peter Firmin went on to create ITV's long-running **Musical Box** in 1959. "They asked me to think of a fifteen minute programme which could be made for £50," says Firmin, "and I came up with the idea of animating nursery rhymes. I did it for eight years in all, first with Rolf Harris, then with Wally Whyton. I've still

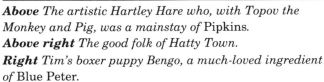

Above The artistic Hartley Hare who, with Topov the Monkey and Pig, was a mainstay of Pipkins.
Above right The good folk of Hatty Town.
Right Tim's boxer puppy Bengo, a much-loved ingredient of Blue Peter.

got some discs of Rolf and I singing in little voices at double speed to sound like cats and foxes."

Another Postgate/Firmin creation was **The Seal of Neptune**, the underwater adventures of a seahorse and a shrimp.

A contemporary of *Rainbow* in the early seventies was ATV's **Pipkins**, starring Hartley Hare with human support from Wayne Laryea. Hartley became an unlikely pin-up, being besieged with cards on his birthday. The hand up Hartley was that of Nigel Plaskitt, who at the time was much loved for playing Malcolm, the poor lad who had to take his exams with a cold in the Vicks Sinex commercials. These days Plaskitt works grown-up puppets in *Spitting Image*. It's a long way from Hartley Hare to the Pope.

Unfortunately, Hartley was not appreciated by everyone who worked on the show. One director, after a long, tiring day in the studio, was heard to describe the furry star adored by thousands as "nothing but a bloody oven glove." It takes a particularly fragile artistic temperament to fall out with a glove puppet... ✴

Chapter 3

"We belong together"

In 1958, an impoverished former film cutting room assistant teamed up with four colleagues to make puppet films in a converted Slough warehouse. They started with just £500 capital and sound proofed the warehouse into a studio by nailing 1,500 empty egg boxes to the walls. That hard up movie man was Gerry Anderson, who was to introduce a new word into television vocabulary — Supermarionation.

Anderson's first project was **The Adventures of Twizzle**, a Roberta Leigh story about a character who could stretch his arms and legs to enormous lengths. It is not known whether this facility applied to any other part of his anatomy. Twizzle's sidekick was an irritating cat with a silly voice and huge paws called Footso. Fifty-two episodes of *Twizzle* were followed by the same number of adventures about **Torchy the Battery Boy** who, as his name implies, was battery operated. Torchy was an innocuous soul, forever bullied by an awful girl called Bossy Boots. There was also Pom Pom the poodle, who insisted on having her hair curled each night.

The year 1960 brought **Four Feather Falls**, a puppet western starring Sheriff Tex Tucker with his two magic guns, Pedro the Bandit, Chief Kalamakooya, and a talking horse and dog, Rocky and Dusty. Tex's special powers were the result of four feathers given to him by an Indian. One feather gave the power of speech to Rocky, another to Dusty and the other two made his guns fire automatically whenever his life was in danger. Even Cheyenne Bodie was no match for Tex Tucker.

This was the breakthrough series for Anderson, with sophisticated new techniques including puppet wires only 1/5,000th of an inch thick and therefore hardly visible — a far cry from the days of *Andy Pandy*. For added realism, the characters' lip movements were synchronised electrically. Tex's voice was provided by Nicholas Parsons, but thankfully when the cowboy burst into song popular crooner Michael Holliday took over.

Anderson's first venture into space came

Above *Twizzle would go to great lengths to avoid being seen with Footso the cat.*
Left *Pork to starboard. Captain John Slater with able seamen Pinky and Perky.*

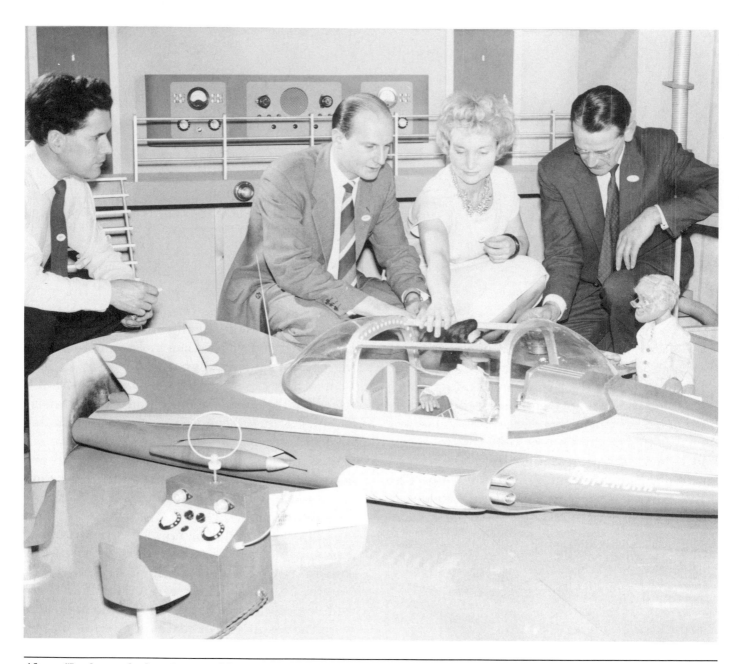

Above *"Look out, the boss is around," warns Mike Mercury as Gerry Anderson inspects Supercar.*

the following year with **Supercar**, a versatile craft that could travel anywhere in the world — over land, through the air and in the sea — although it would undoubtedly have drawn the line at the M25 in rush hour. Now with the backing of Sir Lew Grade, Anderson improved further on the techniques used in *Four Feather Falls* with the result that the series was sold to over forty countries. Anderson's company needed Lew's backing — Supercar itself cost £1,000 to build.

The show's hero was test pilot Mike Mercury. He fought evil with the help of ten year-old Jimmy Gibson (whose voice was provided by Gerry Anderson's wife Sylvia) and his talking monkey Mitch. Other goodies were Supercar's inventor Professor Popkiss and his assistant, the stammering Dr Beaker, while enemy forces were led by Masterspy and his oily accomplice Zarin.

Supercar's successor was **Fireball XL5**, the series for which the term 'Supermarionation' was first used. Set in 2063, it featured the interplanetary adventures of a spacecraft piloted by Steve Zodiac, a 20" tall Adonis, and his crew — blonde space doctor Venus and navigator Mat

Above The crew of Fireball XL5, which had a detachable nose cone for landings called Fireball Junior.
Below Stingray had sixteen missiles to combat Titan's deadly Terror Fish.

STINGRAY CHARACTERS

Troy Tempest
Lt George 'Phones' Sheridan
Marina
Commander Sam Shore
Atlanta
Sub-Lieutenant Fisher
Titan
Agent X20

Matic. The 300' long XL5 was part of a World Space Fleet run by Commander Zero and also had its own pet, a creature called the Lazoon which devoured Martian Delight.

The Andersons' next project was **Stingray**, an atomic powered submarine captained by the 'strikingly handsome' Troy Tempest, very much the Arnold Schwarzenegger of his day. Tempest worked for WASP (the World Aquanaut Security Patrol), an organisation dedicated to making the oceans of the world safe from the threat of the demonic Titan and his army of mechanical Terror Fish. Troy's companions were the mute Marina, just about the prettiest green-haired girl around at the time, and hydrophone opera-

tor Lieutenant George 'Phones' Sheridan. The underwater sequences in *Stingray* were filmed through a tank containing real fish, the puppets being placed behind the tank.

But the *pièce de résistance* of the Super-marionation world arrived in 1965 with **Thunderbirds**, featuring the exploits of International Rescue, a futuristic crime-fighting outfit run by former astronaut Jeff Tracy and his five sons, each named after the first five

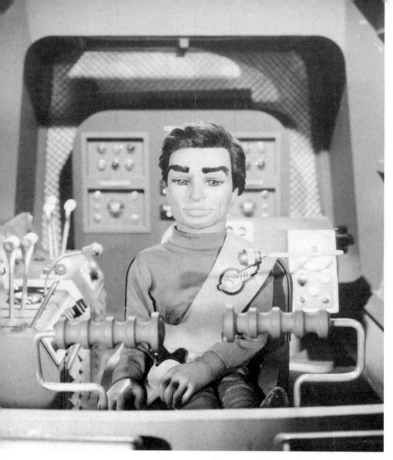

Americans in space. The silver-grey Thunderbird 1 attained speeds of 7,000mph and was piloted by the eldest son Scott; Thunderbird 2 was a huge green freighter manned by Virgil; Thunderbird 3 was orange and the responsibility of one time ace racing driver Alan (he was a real hunk); and Thunderbird 4, a yellow underwater craft, was controlled by Gordon, the youngest son who was something of an impetuous youth.

All four craft were based at International Rescue's hideaway on a remote Pacific island where the cliff face and trees retreated and a swimming pool disappeared so that the Thunderbirds could enter and leave under a cloak of secrecy. And all the time John Tracy waited in space in Thunderbird 5, hoping to

Left Scott in a moment of intense concentration at the controls of Thunderbird 2.
Below Whose life could have been complete without a Thunderbirds *jigsaw in the sixties?*

catch elusive villain The Hood, a sinister master of disguise.

The team also comprised Brains, a bespectacled scientific genius, and Lady Penelope, International Rescue's glamorous blonde London agent who was driven around in a pink, gadget-laden Rolls-Royce (number plate FAB 1) by her Cockney chauffeur, a reformed safeblower named Parker. These two stole the show, particularly with Parker's subservient, much imitated "Yus, m'lady." Sylvia Anderson provided the voice for Lady P who, like the other puppets, cost £300 to make. And they all had a selection of heads to reflect their different moods. It was hard to tell with Jeff Tracy, who always looked bland. For although he had courage, wealth and an immaculate hairstyle, the fact remained that he had the personality of a double glazing salesman and a walk that was only marginally less silly than that of Spotty Dog.

Thunderbirds was also remarkable for being the first British TV series to fully exploit its merchandising. Aside from the now obligatory annuals, records (including the *Thunderbirds Are Go!* EP by Cliff and The Shadows), toys, stationery, bubblegum cards and enough confectionery to rot several sets of teeth, there were some more unusual items. Lady Penelope was

Above *Surprisingly, the* Thunderbirds *soundtrack records didn't threaten the Beatles chart supremacy.*
Below *"Yus, m'lady". Parker and Lady Penelope in their shocking pink Rolls Royce, FAB 1.*

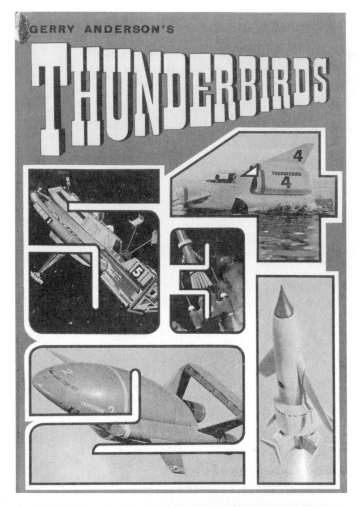

singled out with Lady Penelope dollie dressmaker sets, Lady Penelope dressing table sets and Lady Penelope kites. There was even a *Thunderbirds* watering can in the style of Thunderbird 2 and a Thunderbird 1 shaped radio. Such was the programme's popularity, some of these items originated from as far afield as Japan and Australia.

More substantial spinoffs included two feature films, *Thunderbirds Are Go!* and *Thunderbird 6*. And just before *Thunderbirds* was aired, we were treated to the great children's comic *TV21*, the number 1 Universe Edition appearing on 23 January 1965, although actually dated 2065. The front cover resembled a newspaper, and early strips included *Fireball XL5*, *Supercar*, *Stingray*, *Lady Penelope*, *My Favourite Martian* and *The Daleks*.

The next production, **Captain Scarlet and the Mysterons**, cost a cool £1,500,000 and related the struggle of the gallant, indestructible Captain Scarlet and his squad of colour coded Spectrum agents to outwit Martian foes the Mysterons, who were hell-bent on destroying mankind. Well, it's a living. Leading baddie was the sinister Captain Black, an ex-Spectrum agent who had been taken over by the Mysterons during an expedition to Mars. As well as being indestructible, Captain Scarlet was aided in his task by some ace machines, particularly the five-seater Spectrum Saloon and the bullet-proof Spectrum Pursuit Vehicle (SPV), capable of speeds of up to 200mph.

Whereas the earlier marionettes possessed the largest heads since the heyday of Matt Monro, the figures for Captain Scarlet, Colonel White, Captain Black and co were perfectly proportioned. And the eyes were those of production company employees which were photographed and then superimposed on to plastic eyeballs.

Gerry Anderson's ninth puppet show saw a return to *terra firma*. **Joe 90**, a nine year-old schoolboy with big glasses, was the adopted son of Professor Ian McClaine, creator of BIG RAT (Brain Impulse Galvanoscope Record and

Top Five! Four! Three! Two! One! Thunderbirds are go!
Left International Rescue, headquarters of Thunderbirds.

CAPTAIN SCARLET CHARACTERS

Captain Scarlet	Colonel White
Captain Blue	Captain Grey
Captain Ochre	Captain Magenta
Lt Green	Dr Fawn

Captain Black

The Angels (Symphony, Melody, Rhapsody, Harmony, Destiny)

Above *The eyes had it on* Captain Scarlet and the Mysterons. **Left** *Joe 90 prepares to be transformed from schoolboy to secret agent in BIG RAT.*

Transfer). McClaine, whose voice came courtesy of Rupert (*Maigret*) Davies, used his invention on Joe, transforming him into the World Intelligence Network's top agent. One minute the lad was behind his desk learning his twelve times table, the next he was a brain surgeon. That's what I call a YTS scheme!

Although Gerry Anderson virtually monopolised sixties sci-fi puppet shows, Roberta Leigh (creator of *Twizzle* and *Torchy*) did weigh in with **Space Patrol**, which starred such luminaries as Captain Larry Dart, Husky the Martian and Slim the Venusian. They were members of the United Galactic Organisation set up to keep the peace between the planets in the year 2100. But in the face of competition from *Fireball XL5*, their efforts went largely unnoticed. There were simply too many people trying to save the world at the time.

Fred Barker and Ollie Beak had no such pretensions — they were more interested in spreading anarchy than peace and goodwill. The pair were regular ingredients of ITV's **Small**

Time, along with Sarah and Hoppity, Snoozy the sea-lion with Dorothy Smith, and Theodore the rabbit with Larry Parker.

Fred and Ollie were created by Oliver Postgate and Peter Firmin. Shaggy dog Fred began life in a show called **Dogwatch**, set in a lighthouse, and his voice was provided by Ivan Owen, the man who went on to put the "Boom Boom" into Basil Brush. Oliver Postgate, who had been at drama school with Owen, remembers: "Ivan found that by sitting underneath a puppet out of vision, he could get away with far more than he could if he were seen. Camera rehearsals between Fred and Ollie were chaos. There was no script — Ivan and Wally Whyton

(who did Ollie) just said whatever they liked. They were blue, there was outrageous political comment, the lot. New young directors were known to age visibly at their repartee and had to be assured that it would all be perfectly safe at transmission time."

Skiffle singer Wally Whyton based Scouse owl Ollie on his own younger brother. Ollie's feathers were plucked from a real Rhode Island Red and whenever he was getting threadbare, Whyton's co-presenter Muriel Young used to ring her friends and ask for more. Whyton says: "I had this horrible feeling of a chicken being killed every time Ollie needed new feathers!"

In those days, Wally and Muriel had to ad lib in the continuity suites between programmes if there weren't sufficient commercials. This could last anything up to eight minutes. Whyton recalls one New Year's Day when there were no

adverts. "Ollie Beak came in with a balloon and announced, 'I've been to the Chelsea Owls' Ball.' To which Muriel replied innocently, 'I didn't know owls had balls.' I don't know how we carried on without cracking up completely."

But despite the wit of Fred and Ollie, for some unaccountable reason the star of *Small Time* — and didn't he know it! — was **Pussy Cat Willum**. I have to admit that I actively hated Pussy Cat Willum. He was the type of cat that made you think Little Johnny Green had the right idea. He was quite the most objectionable glove puppet I have ever encountered, insufferably smug with a definite air of arrogance. I longed to pull out his stuffing, piece by piece. I'm sure Ollie Beak must have loathed him too and probably gave him a sly peck when they were off camera. Yet Willum achieved superstar status, receiving as many as 400 letters a week. Then again, Hitler had his followers too...

Wally Whyton, still a leading light in the folk music world, is unrepentant about having worked with Willum. "Some people say to me, 'Weren't you embarrassed about doing all those kids' shows on TV?' Why should I be? After all, I got a house out of Pussy Cat Willum."

Following his success with Ollie and Fred, ITV approached Peter Firmin to come up with some new puppets for a series called **The**

and Ollie Beak. You can
them every Tuesday and Fri-

Above *The delightful Muriel Young takes care not to ruffle Ollie's feathers.*
Left *Fred tells Howard Williams a shaggy dog story.*
Below *Pussy Cat Willum is unimpressed by Wally Whyton's jokes.*

Three Scampies. They suggested tiger cubs but Firmin fancied the idea of a fox with a Terry-Thomas voice. **Basil Brush** was born.

The Three Scampies were Howard Williams, Scottish hedgehog Spike McPike and Basil. "It cost me £12 to make Basil and Spike," recalls Firmin, "and I got a deal whereby I was paid £1 for each time Basil appeared on TV." Ivan Owen supplied the famous voice and it was he who decided to take Basil to the BBC after the puppet had been curled up in Peter Firmin's bottom drawer for six months. Success followed swiftly, first on *The David Nixon Show* and then in 1968 in Basil's own BBC series. Owen reportedly went on to make £1,000,000 out of the character. Basil's adventures have been translated into Japanese and Afrikaans and in

Trivia

Basil Brush

BASIL BRUSH'S STRAIGHT MEN

Rodney Bewes   Derek Fowlds
Roy North   Billy Boyle
Howard Williams

Above *Spike McPike and Basil Brush, two of* The Three Scampies.

Germany he is known as 'Balduin Schwupp'. The Americans didn't take the series but wanted to change his name for the books. "They said Basil wasn't a very good name for a macho character," says Firmin, "but I resisted."

Basil was my kind of puppet (not like that wimp Orville), always ready with a wisecrack and a quick put down at the expense of his human partner, inevitably followed by a resounding "BOOM! BOOM!" It required a defi-

nite discipline to play straight man to Basil, as the likes of Rodney Bewes, Derek Fowlds and Roy North will testify. Whenever I see Derek Fowlds in a high-powered drama it is hard not to hark back to the days when he stood alongside a stuffed fox who prodded him with his snout and called him Mr Derek. That was the stuff of which BAFTA Awards are really made.

Roy North was Basil's longest serving stooge, the pair making four series together from 1973. "It was the first time I'd ever worked with a puppet," says North, "and I soon realised that the only way to make it work was to treat Basil as a real person. We had a good rapport. He liked to surprise me with ad libs in rehearsals, but I remember once when the joke was on him. We had these pet mice in the studio and they started crawling up Basil. He didn't know what to do. I was supposed to be doing the end song, 'Blast Off Basil', but I just couldn't carry on. I fell about laughing.

"I suppose you could say that was Basil's boom boom time, because we kicked off Saturday evening's entertainment and pulled in audiences of 11,000,000. And even today some people still call me 'Mr Roy'."

In the early fifties, Ivan Owen had been behind Yoo-Hoo the cuckoo on one of television's first puppet shows, **Billy Bean and His**

Above One of children's television's finest double acts - Roy North and Basil Brush.

Funny Machine. Billy's machine was a wonder to behold, featuring such devices as a windmill, a Dorset-Faucet and a cartoonerator which drew magic pictures. Also popular at that time were Timothy Telescope and Cactus the Camel, who used to appear with Valerie Hobson on **Telescope**, and Alison Uttley's stories of **The Little Grey Rabbit**, illustrated by the puppets of Jan Bussell and Ann Hogarth.

In 1954, Goon Michael Bentine introduced **The Bumblies**, three pear-shaped creatures from the planet Bumble. The star of the show was the hard-of-thinking Bumbley number three, a creation in the mould of Eccles. Many years later, Bentine came up with another children's classic, **Potty Time**, and if you were allowed to stay up late, there was nothing better in the sixties than his inventive models for **It's a Square World**. Even at the age of eleven, there was something very pleasurable about

Above Billy Bean is greeted by Yoo-Hoo the cuckoo. The Funny Machine was devised by Chuck Luchsinger.

watching the House of Commons being blown up.

Larry the Lamb and his friends transferred **Toytown** to television, complete with an enormous Mayor, Peter Brough did the same with Archie Andrews in **Educating Archie** (Dick Emery was a regular guest), Jean Morton invited us to join the **Tingha and Tucker Club** (remember their greeting, "Hullo, Auntie Jean"?) and Terry Hall wielded the incomparable **Lenny the Lion**, a somewhat camp King of the jungle who couldn't roll his 'r's and who had wide eyes and a habit of putting his huge paw to his head and sighing, "Don't embawass me."

The idea came to Terry Hall while watching a particularly languid lion at Blackpool Zoo. "I already had a boy dummy, Mickey Flynn, but impressario Val Parnell said that all ventriloquists used wooden boy dummies and that I

Left Hedgehog the milkman makes a special delivery to Little Grey Rabbit.
Below Michael Bentine in command of his manic masterpiece, Potty Time.

should try for something different. So after going to the zoo I thought of a soppy lion character, and singer Anne Shelton, with whom I was on stage at the time, suggested the voice." The

first Lenny was made by a Madame Tussaud's employee in 1954 and, incredibly, in the ensuing thirty-seven years there have only ever been two puppets. "Right at the start I tried to get a duplicate made," says Hall, "in case Lenny was pinched from the back of my car. After all, without him my livelihood would have gone. But the chap who made the original found it impossible to come up with a twin and it was a while before I was

Above The visitor explains that he was calling the metamorphosed Mayor of Toytown 'pig', not P.C. Ernest. **Below** 'Auntie' Jean Morton with cuddly Koalas Tingha and Tucker. But where's Willy Wombat?

Above *David Bowie's favourite, Lenny the Lion, seen here with his master, Terry Hall.*

able to obtain an identical lookalike."

What made Lenny different was that he was the first ventriloquist's puppet to have arm movements. He took off in a big way and soon earned his own show. "I decided to set up a fan club for Lenny," says Hall. "I thought it would just be a steady trickle but there were 500 applicants a week. It was all too much for me to run so it was taken over by Haywood Jones of Dr Barnardo's. Haywood had a son, David, aged about eight, who used to come along to all Lenny's shows. Haywood said that young David was very keen on getting into the music business and asked me whether I could offer any advice. I was staggered to discover later that little David Jones had become David Bowie!"

Fancy that, Bowie being a closet Lenny the Lion fan. A lad insane...?

Lenny's other brush with the rock world came with his series *Pops and Lenny* which began in 1962. Here I can reveal that The Beatles were once the support act to Lenny the Lion.

"The Beatles had just had their first hit when they were guests on the show," recalls Terry Hall. "Lenny and I had the number one dressing room, because it was our show, and The Beatles were in number two. But because they had such a large *entourage*, they asked if Lenny and I would mind sharing, which was no problem. I always did a comedy routine with Lenny immediately before the guest star's spot, but on this occasion the moment the tabs went up behind me and all the kids in the audience saw The Beatles I had to wind up there and then. I couldn't continue. I just introduced them and got off. I remember afterwards my daughter came backstage to see me as usual and because I was sharing with the boys, she saw The Beatles getting changed. When she went to school the next day she proudly told everyone that she had seen The Beatles in their underwear!"

Now sixty-five, Terry Hall lives in Coventry, which coincidentally is the home town of the other showbiz Terry Hall, the former lead singer with The Specials and Fun Boy Three. I wonder how many good citizens of Coventry have gone expecting to see a Specials concert and ended up spending an evening with Lenny the Lion.

In 1957, two little pigs with speeded-up voices started hamming it up on BBC. They were **Pinky and Perky**, the creation of Czechs Jan and Vlasta Dalibor who smuggled themselves into Britain in 1948. Jan was a painter and sculptor and Vlasta an actress. "I had always been interested in puppets," says Jan, "and Vlasta suggested I make some puppet pigs because the pig is a symbol of good luck in

---

Below *I Wanna Hold Your Beak. Half of The Beakles from* Pinky and Perky. *Note Paul's left-handed guitar.*

Czechoslovakia. I came up with twin boy pigs — Pinky who wore red and Perky who wore blue." Since most of the shows were in black and white, the only sure way to tell them apart was that Perky was the one in the hat.

Their programmes were originally intended purely for children's television, but as they pranced around to the hit sounds of the sixties the little porkers received the accolade of promotion to a more adult viewing hour. They attracted more viewers than the hideously popular American import *The Lucy Show* with Lucille Ball and even hit the big time in the States, making six appearances on the prestigious *Ed Sullivan Show* and doing a year at the gaming capital of the world, Las Vegas. Pinky and Perky were real backgammon...

The Americans loved them — so much so that when Ambrose Cat's head fell off in the middle of a rendition of Elvis's 'Jailhouse Rock', the audience thought it was all part of the act

Above John Slater points an offensive weapon in the direction of Pinky and Perky.
Right Basil Bloodhound, ace cameraman at PPC TV.

and applauded wildly.

The Dalibors were quick to realise the potential of a sort of Pork Box Jury and music came to dominate the shows. Pinky and Perky ran their own television station, PPC TV, where they were joined by Jimmy Thompson (other human partners were Roger Moffat, John Slater, Brian Burdon and the outsize Fred Emney). Their theme song was the catchy 'We Belong Together' and they even introduced a group called The Beakles which, as their name implies, consisted of a fab four with huge beaks — a sight which must have been somewhat disconcerting for Ringo.

Incredibly, at the height of their fame, Pinky and Perky received almost as much fan mail as the real Beatles! Ardent admirers sent them scarfs, mittens, cardigans and cakes.

In all, the Dalibors had some fifty puppets. Besides Pinky and Perky and Ambrose Cat, there was Horace Hare (the spitting image of Ken Dodd), Basil Bloodhound, Morton Frog, Conchita the Cow with her long eyelashes, Bertie the baby elephant and the sultry Vera Vixen, who looked like a cross between Eartha Kitt and Basil Brush — plus a seemingly endless supply of mice.

Human guest stars included Michael Aspel, Stratford Johns (in 'Z Pigs'), Freddie and the Dreamers and Henry Cooper.

To everyone else, *Pinky and Perky* seemed harmless fun — but not to the BBC. They banned the programme in 1966 for being too political. The Dalibors had planned a programme titled 'You Too Can Be a Prime Minister' but, fearful of any political content with a general election approaching, the BBC decided to postpone transmission until after polling day. However, there was such a public outcry that they promptly reinstated it. Jimmy Thompson couldn't understand what all the fuss was about. He said at the time: "All that happens is I stand for election, have cabbages

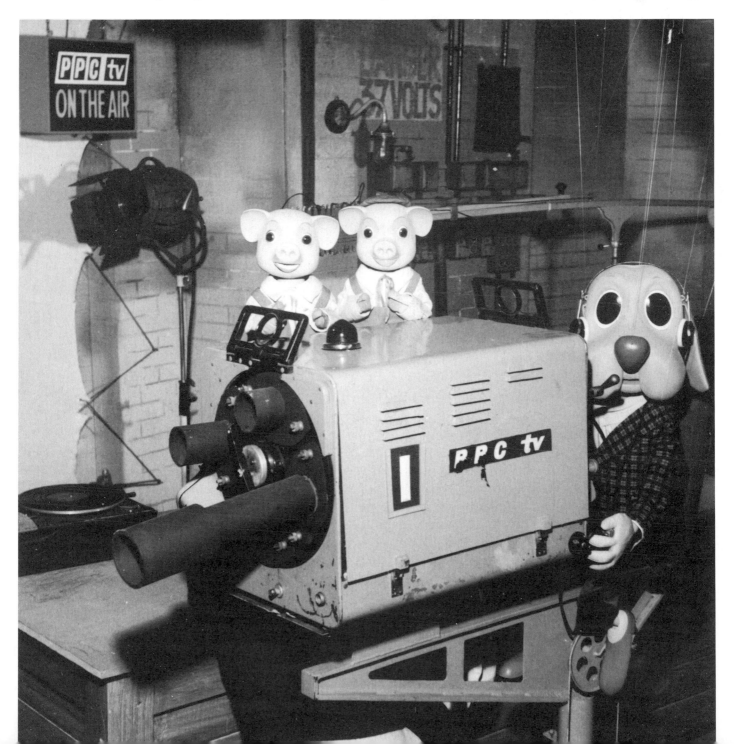

thrown at me and when I eventually arrive at Number Ten, I find Pinky and Perky already there." Maybe it was a bit too close to reality after all.

Jan Dalibor recalls: "Ironically, when 'You Too Can Be a Prime Minister' was finally shown, it attracted more viewers than Harold Wilson's party political broadcast which was on ITV at the same time."

PINKY AND PERKY'S SONGS

Their cover versions included:

Rawhide
White Horses
When I'm 64
Yellow Submarine
The Runaway Train
All My Loving
Rockinghorse Cowboy
Hello Dolly

The great thing about puppets is that they're much easier to train than real animals. Apart from the occasional broken string, which would make Pinky look less perky than usual, Jan Dalibor reports no great disasters with the puppets. "But we did have a few problems when we used live animals on the show. I remember a St Bernard that was supposed to perform a mountain rescue. He was very placid, but the moment the studio lights went on the buzz caused him to howl uncontrollably. In the end

Left Pinky and Perky may look in charge of the ship, but Vlasta and Jan Dalibor are pulling the strings.

Above Guess who's coming to dinner? Bertie Bonkers the baby elephant.
Below Pinky and Perky's kitchen. Sausages are off.

we had to shoot the scene with reduced lighting. Another time we had a racehorse which was bringing Pinky and Perky back to the studio from the races. Unfortunately, just before the take this highly tuned thoroughbred fell asleep!"

Above Gus Honeybun, still a star of Television South-West.
Left Lamb Chop tests Shari Lewis's breath for suspicious traces of mint sauce.
Below left The voice of Topo Gigio came courtesy of Keith Alexander, who also spoke for Sam Loover in Joe 90.
Below right The Telegoons proved that if you split a single brain cell, you'd be left with Eccles and Bluebottle.

Above *Tich and Quackers are grateful they didn't go to the same hairdresser as Ray Allan.*

After a brief stint with Thames, Pinky and Perky retired in 1970. But they have recently cavorted back into the limelight on video. It's good to know that, as far as the Dalibors are concerned, they are still bringing home the bacon.

Other puppet favourites from the Golden Age were **Shari Lewis with Lamb Chop**, the south-west's very own **Gus Honeybun**, who's still doing bunny hops to celebrate a birthday, **Ken Dodd's Diddymen**, **Topo Gigio**, the Italian mouse with the big ears and the Des O'Connor dimple, and **The Telegoons**, based on the famous *Goon Show* from the radio. At last viewers could see in the sort-of-flesh the likes of Eccles, Bluebottle, Moriarty, Neddy Seagoon, Min and Henry, Grytpype-Thynne and Major Dennis Bloodnok. Wonderful stuff.

Master ventriloquist Ray Allan, who began with Mikki the Martian, went on to team a naughty schoolboy **Tich** with a 'daft duck' **Quackers**. The result was great entertainment and worse puns than you heard in the fourth form. The put upon Quackers was a true star — he could see off today's pale imitation, Edd the Duck, with one wing behind his back. And the early seventies introduced **Rod Hull and Emu**, to whom the nation will always owe a debt of gratitude simply for getting his beak around Michael Parkinson where it hurts.

But I have left the real puppet superstar until last — a chap who could have reduced Troy Tempest to a quivering wreck with just one squirt of his water pistol. I refer, of course, to the much-loved **Sooty**.

At the grand old age of forty-three, Sooty has outlived such luminaries as James Dean, Henry V, Marilyn Monroe, Rudolph Valentino and Alexander the Great. He has long been a British institution, hailed as the last great silent star. His contribution to society has not gone unnoticed. His creator, the late Harry

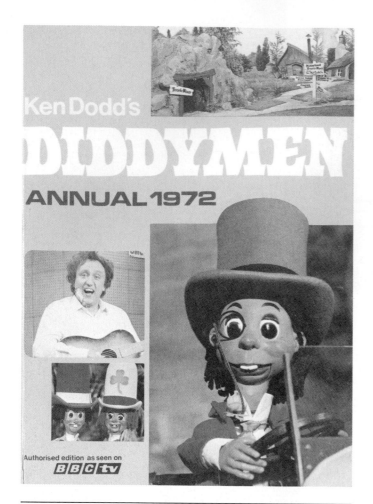

Above *Nigel Ponsonby-Smallpiece fronts the 1972 Diddymen Annual.*

SOME OF DODDY'S DIDDYMEN FROM KNOTTY ASH

Dicky Mint
Mick the Marmaliser
Nigel Ponsonby-Smallpiece
Hamish McDiddy
Evan

Corbett, was awarded the O.B.E. (a special mini gong was made for Sooty), while in his foreword to my book, *The Secret Life of Sooty*, no less a person than George Harrison wrote: 'Sooty is proof that sanity is still with us.'

The Sooty story began in 1948 when, on a wet family holiday in Blackpool, Yorkshire engineer and part-time magician Harry Corbett spotted a glove puppet teddy bear in a novelty shop at the end of the North pier. "I'd always had a thing about teddy bears," said Harry, "and this one had a cheeky face. It was almost as if it was saying, 'Don't leave me here.' " So Harry splashed out 7s 6d and took the little bear back to the boarding house in a brown paper bag.

Harry incorporated the bear into his magic act and their fame spread until, in 1952, they made their television debut on a BBC show called *Talent Night*. They were an instant success. *The Sunday Express* of 4 May enthused: 'Five minutes on the television screen last night established Harry Corbett's teddy bear as a rival to Muffin the Mule.' At that stage the puppet was just known as teddy and had decidedly sharp features. Harry's widow Marjorie says it looked like a rat! The Corbetts were advised to give it a more distinctive look and, above all, a name. They experimented by making it all black, which didn't work. But then they hit on the idea of blacking only its ears and nose with soot from the chimney. The result was Sooty.

Harry was so confident of success that at the age of thirty-four he gave up his day job to turn full-time and appear in the BBC children's series *Saturday Special* which starred comedian Peter Butterworth, later a stalwart of the Carry On films. As Harry and Sooty went from strength to strength, soon earning their own show, Harry even took the precaution of paying £150 a year to insure the thumb and first two fingers of his right hand for £20,000. He acknowledged that those limbs were his fortune — he was the original Goldfinger.

Harry's own character was to become almost as important as that of the mischievous bear. How we loved to see poor old Harry's face covered in ink or flour, or sometimes both, the victim of another of Sooty's pranks, while he donned that harassed, brow-beaten look to utter those familiar closing words: "Bye bye everybody. Bye bye."

Not everybody enjoyed Harry's antics

Right *Sooty's infamous balsa wood hammer leaves its mark on poor Harry Corbett.*

though — the BBC wardrobe department for one. It was their job to clean his suits, but they called a halt after one particularly messy episode. Harry remembered: "I always used to wear a good suit, because if you wore overalls the kids would know right at the start that something messy was going to happen and it wouldn't be as funny. One time I was covered in a pound bag of flour and two eggs. My suit was in a right state but I peeled it off and took it along to wardrobe as usual. But when I returned to collect it two weeks later, it was still bundled up in a corner where I'd left it.

Attached to it was a curt note which read: 'In future please take your suits back home and clean them yourself.'

"After that I started taking them to a cleaner in Bradford. Every week I'd turn up with a suit plastered with raw egg and flour. The manager thought I was a raving lunatic!"

There were other scrapes. On one show, Sooty, aiming for Harry, squirted Janet Brown with black water paint. Not only was Janet wearing a light coloured gown which she had bought for £100 specially for the programme but she was just about to sing her solo number. She had no option but to warble in a paint-spattered dress. Sooty also risked royal wrath by squirting Prince Philip with his water pistol at a trade fair. He was probably only spared a night in the Tower by the fact that young Princess Anne was said to be a big Sooty fan.

But while the water pistol survived, Sooty's other favourite prop, the little balsa wood hammer, didn't. BBC children's television supremo Freda Lingstrom disapproved of the hammer, claiming it set a bad example to youngsters. The last straw was a story about a man who was quietly reading his Sunday paper when his son whacked him over the head with a real hammer — so forcibly that he had to go to hospital to have stitches put in the wound.

The boy's mum said: "Why did you do that to daddy?"

Above "Bye bye everybody," squeaked Sweep.
Left Sooty's expertise at the xylophone was no fluke - Harry Corbett was a trained classical pianist.

"Well, Sooty did it," replied the son.

In 1957 Sooty was joined by Sweep, a dim dog with a sausage fetish. Together they were a superb double act, the Morecambe and Wise of glove puppets — Sooty with his xylophone, magic wand, oofle dust and spells of "Izzy whizzy, let's get busy" and Sweep with his endless supply of bones.

Seven years later, Harry decided to intro-duce another character — Soo, a little panda girlfriend for Sooty. The BBC were not amused and banned Soo on the grounds that her inclusion would bring sex into children's television! After a huge outcry, they eventually relented but only on condition that Sooty and Soo must never touch...

Other new arrivals were Ramsbottom, the snake with a broad Yorkshire accent, Kipper the cat and Butch, a fierce dog who made a rottweiller look like a toy poodle. The show even went on tour to large theatres, where a woman in the audience once complained to the manager that she couldn't hear a word that Sooty was saying to Mr Corbett. When the story was duly relayed to Harry, he said: "Go and tell her neither can I."

It seemed like the end of the road for Sooty when, along with Pinky and Perky, he was axed in the BBC purge of 1968, but The Sooteries was rebuilt at Thames Television. One casualty, though, was Harry's brother Leslie who had operated Sweep but was unable to get time off from his job with the Electricity Board in Yorkshire to travel down to Teddington for the shows. Leslie was so distraught at losing Sweep that he had to be treated for depression.

His place was taken by Harry's son Matthew, who on one show had the misfortune to lay out Gerry Marsden of Gerry and the Pacemakers fame. Matthew was supposed to hit Gerry with a mallet which had a harmless polyurethane head, but he missed and instead it was the mallet's wooden handle that crashed down on Gerry's unsuspecting skull. Gerry was out cold — Matthew thought he'd killed him. Gerry went to hospital to have sixteen stitches inserted in the wound, but worst of all he had to tell the doctor that he had been knocked out on *The Sooty Show*.

At 3.30am on Christmas Day, 1975, Harry Corbett suffered a massive heart attack and although he eventually recovered, was too weak to carry on with Sooty full time. His son Matthew took over and is still running the show today.

Harry, who died in 1989, was devoted to Sooty. He regarded him as a child, one of the family. He would never allow Sooty to be thrown about and, even after a hard day at the studio, he didn't bully him at home. He never exacted revenge for a good soaking by using Sooty to wipe the dinner dishes. What's more, Harry always kept his nails short — much to Sooty's relief.

The Corbetts always took Sooty on holiday. Once Harry turned back when he realised they had forgotten him. And when he travelled, he was laid out reverentially on a piece of cloth — always face up — in a box with airholes, so that he could breathe properly!

Over the years there have been more than 1,000 Sootys in all, but Harry only ever thought of there being one. Shortly before he died, Harry said: "I often found myself wondering what he was thinking. It was as bad as that. Before every show, I washed his face and brushed his fur. If I accidentally dropped him, I immediately apologised. I know it sounds ridiculous regarding Sooty as a person because he was really only two fingers on my right hand, but I can't help it. The worst thing was having to break in a new

Above Tucking Sooty into bed was Harry's favourite routine - but from his face you'd never think it.

Sooty puppet. I used to think of it as a new partner who didn't know me yet. I got so anxious, I used to come out in beads of sweat. And I felt terrible about the one I had just discarded — I used to apologise to them and say, 'I'm sorry but I'm not using you again.' I'm so bloody soft at times."

Besides the Soo sex scandal, in his time

Sooty has been accused of pushing drugs (after Sweep was placed in a tranquilising booth) and being anti-police (a storybook showed him attempting to hit PC Nab with a hammer). Yet he has maintained a dignified silence throughout, preferring to keep a low profile. Did you ever see Sooty at the head of an anti-Vietnam demonstration? Did Harry Corbett ever emulate John Lennon and claim that Sooty was more popular than Jesus? Of course not. What's more, in a showbusiness world rife with jealousy and failed relationships, I can reveal that Sooty, Sweep and Soo were good pals off screen too. There is absolutely no truth in the rumour that Soo once ditched Sooty for one of the Wombles.

It has been a glorious career, best summed up by Harry Corbett's widow Marjorie, who some years ago offered this profound judgment on her husband's chosen lifestyle. "Harry is the only man I know who can stick his hand up a bear's backside, wiggle its ears and make money." Say no more. ✳

Chapter 4

"Get down, Shep"

eople can argue about why Roger Whittaker whistles, they can debate the contribution made to the European Community by *It's a Knockout* and dispute that any of the original Cliff Adams Singers can still be on *Sing Something Simple*. But there can be no doubt as to which television programme has done more for the sales of sticky-backed plastic than any other — **Blue Peter**.

Val must have bought the stuff by the yard. I always had visions of her entire house being decorated in sticky-backed plastic and of her watching television on a set made from an old cornflake packet and the tops of four detergent bottles. But I was a little concerned that she always had such a plentiful supply of used toilet rolls. She must have got through an inordinate amount — it quite put me off trying any of her recipes.

Blue Peter has been a way of life for thirty-three years and is currently viewed as an innocent outpost in a world of vigilante turtles and killer tomatoes. Of course there have been scandals, particularly in more recent years. Remember the stories about presenter Michael Sundin's gay nightclub act, Simon Groom eulogising over a couple of door ornaments ("What a beautiful pair of knockers") and Janet Ellis announcing on the programme that she was about to become an unmarried mum? It was one she'd made earlier.

Left Joey the parrot prepares to do a Blue Peter *guest spot on Chris Trace's head.*

The brainchild of John Hunter Blair, *Blue Peter* began transmission on 16 October 1958. Originally just a seven week experiment, it started out as a fifteen minute programme with items on trains for boys and dolls for girls, interspersed with occasional appearances from Tony Hart telling and drawing stories about Packi

BLUE PETER PRESENTERS

Christopher Trace (1958-67)
Leila Williams (1958-62)
Valerie Singleton (1962-71)
John Noakes (1965-79)
Peter Purves (1967-79)
Lesley Judd (1971-79)
Simon Groom (1978-86)
Christopher Wenner (1979-80)
Tina Heath (1979-80)
Sarah Greene (1980-84)
Peter Duncan (1980-84, 1986)
Michael Sundin (1984-86)
Janet Ellis (1984-87)
Mark Curry (1986-89)
Caron Keating (1986-90)
Yvette Fielding (1987-
John Leslie (1989-
Diane-Louise Jordan (1990-

the baby elephant. Even then, elephants were an integral part of *Blue Peter!* The first presenters were twenty-one year-old Leila Williams, the previous year's Miss Great Britain, and twenty-five year-old former army officer turned actor, Christopher Trace (he had been Charlton Heston's stand-in on *Ben-Hur*). Chris, who was paid five guineas for that first show, remembers: "I got the *Blue Peter* job because I was mad about model railways. In fact I spent the entire interview playing trains with John Hunter Blair. On that first show I wore a suit and Leila wore an afternoon frock."

So, heralded by its jaunty theme 'Barnacle Bill', *Blue Peter* set sail on a voyage of discovery, although John Hunter Blair had to abandon ship after a couple of years, the victim of multiple sclerosis. He later died watching an edition of the programme he had created.

Leila Williams also left after a row with a new producer. "He wanted me to write all my own material," she says. "I told him, 'I'm a presenter, not a writer', and he sacked me." Leila, who married Fred Mudd of the Muddlarks singing group, soon quit showbusiness altogether. She worked as an assistant manageress at Dorothy Perkins in Harrow, before running pubs in Kingston and Surbiton with Fred. Now fifty-four, she confesses: "Fred calls me the granny of *Blue Peter!*"

Her successor was good old Val, a rock-like figure, ideally suited for live television. Long-time *Blue Peter* editor Biddy Baxter once remarked: "If the studio roof had collapsed in the middle of a live programme, Valerie would have stepped out of the rubble and said: 'And now for something quite different', without faltering."

In 1962, Val and Chris were joined by the first in a long line of *Blue Peter* pets. It was Petra, the mongrel puppy who was introduced on the show in a box wrap-

Left *Chris Trace and Leila Williams, the first* Blue Peter *presenters.*

ped in Christmas paper. Alas, two days later the puppy died of distemper and the producers had to hunt round frantically for a lookalike replacement. They found one in a pet shop in Lewisham, South London. Viewers were never told of the switch — as far as they were concerned, there was only ever one Petra. Although Petra II appeared gentle and loving on screen, in reality she was bad tempered with poor eyesight and a shortage of teeth. Chris Trace says: "She would gum you to death if she got half a chance." Nevertheless, Peter Purves was visibly shaken when he announced her death in 1977 and a specially sculpted bronze head of Petra was placed at the entrance of the BBC.

Following the arrival of Petra, the studio was soon awash with pets like Honey the guide dog, Patch (one of Petra's puppies), Jason the Siamese cat, Joey the parrot who, despite constant cajoling from the presenters, steadfastly refused to say "Blue Peter" or anything else on air. I bet Joey let out a stream of Wordsworthian prose once the show had finished. Then there was the tortoise who appeared for two years as Fred before they discovered it was a girl. We eagerly await the arrival of the *Blue Peter* pitbull terrier.

Mention of pets brings me to Shep, the black and white collie, which in turn leads me to the remarkable John Noakes. Complete with a pudding basin haircut which looked as if it had been inflicted by a distant relative of Sweeney Todd, Noakes bounded on to the screen in 1965 and stayed for fifteen memorable years.

Val regularly observed, "Johnny, you're terribly brave", and indeed he was. He climbed Nelson's Column and on another occasion became the first British civilian to make a 25,000ft free-fall descent by parachute. Christopher Trace was only too happy to let him play daredevil. Chris hated heights. He says: "At programme conferences, if it was suggested that we do an item about steeplejacks from the top of a tower, I'd nudge the producer and say, 'That's a Noakes story.' There was no way they were going to get me up there."

Yet for all his bravado, John Noakes was no match for a 5lb imitation marrow. He was knocked out by it during an exhibition of mar-

BLUE PETER PETS

DOGS
Petra	Patch
Honey (mark 1)	Shep
Goldie	Bonnie
Honey (mark 2)	

CATS
Jason	Jack
Jill	Willow

PARROTS
Joey	Barney

TORTOISES
Fred/Freda	Maggie
Jim	George

Above Blue Peter *pets parade - Val with Jason, John with Shep and Peter with Petra.*

row dangling and was taken to hospital for an X-ray.

John's other trait was an unfortunate tendency to forget his lines at the crucial moment. On an item about the Royal Horse Artillery, he suddenly stopped, turned to the Corporal and said: "D'you know what comes next?"

"No sir," said the Corporal.

"Neither do I — and it's getting to be quite a problem."

On another occasion he was presenting a piece about twenty men pedalling a stunt cycle for charity. At the front was Ronnie Barker, and as the familiar face came into view Noakes announced: "And this you'll have no difficulty in recognising as Renny, er Ronnie, Ronnie..."

"Corbett," suggested Barker.

"That's right...no it isn't, is it?"

But his great joy was Shep and his jovial admonition, "Get down, Shep", became a nation-

FAMOUS BLUE PETER APPEALS

1962
Hundreds of sacks of toys made sure that every child in Britain had a Christmas present.

1964
Seven and a half tons of silver paper raised two guide dogs for the blind, Honey and Cindy, plus £125.

1966
240,000 paperback books bought four inshore lifeboats.

1967
750,000,000 used postage stamps provided flats for eight homeless families.

1968
2,000,000 parcels of wool and cotton bought three hospital trucks, six emergency doctor's cars, plus medical equipment to help child victims of the war in Biafra.

1969
500,000 parcels of scrap metal resulted in a variety of equipment to help the disabled.

1975
Over 800 tons of wool and cotton bought twenty-one ponies and helped some 300 centres for handicapped riders.

1979
The Great Bring and Buy Sale Appeal for Cambodia raised £3,710,823.

1982
8,000,000 parcels of treasure (old watch straps, key rings, thimbles, etc) provided vital equipment for children's hospitals.

1984
In the Double Life-Saver Appeal, 6,000,000 envelopes of stamps and over 1,000,000 envelopes of buttons and postcards replaced four *Blue Peter* lifeboats, provided a fifth and helped the famine in Ethiopia.

1989
40,000,000 aluminium cans bought life-support machines, aiding sixty-five hospitals.

1990
The Great Bring and Buy Sale for Romania has so far raised over £6,000,000.

al catchphrase. The pair lived together and went on to further fame in **Go With Noakes**. Alas, they fell out with *Blue Peter* when the BBC refused to allow them to advertise dog food.

The famous *Blue Peter* appeals have raised millions of pounds over the years, with children eagerly sending in old clothes, used stamps, paperback books and milk bottle tops. By 1971 it was estimated that the programme had received seven and a half tons of silver paper. When the programme held a competition to design a train of the future, there were no fewer than 110,000 entrants ranging in age from two to seventy-two. And, of course, it has enjoyed royal patronage. Princess Anne joined Val on the 1971 *Blue Peter* safari to Kenya while a young Prince Edward, who along with his brother Prince Andrew was a great *Blue Peter* fan, popped into the studio to meet a lion cub.

The great thing about *Blue Peter* is that there is never a dull moment — either for the viewers or the presenters. There was once a minor furore over a ginger pop recipe given out on the programme. The Temperance Union claimed it was more than half as alcoholic as beer and described it as a 'dangerously alcoholic brew.' And Christopher Trace remembers some uncomfortable encounters with animals. "I was wee'd on by a seal once, and when we had the biggest pig in England on the show I bent down to give it an apple and split my trousers. I had to pull my sweater down to cover my embarrassment and walk around very carefully, otherwise I'd have put the 'blue' into *Blue Peter*." He certainly earned his *Blue Peter* badge that day.

Chris's passion was the model railways. "It was while constructing the layouts that I invented the phrase 'Here's one I made earlier', because we didn't have instant glue in those days." Others found Chris's layouts a source of

Below left Val dons her Mod gear for the Blue Peter *expedition to Margate. Pity nobody told Peter and John!*
Below right And now for something completely different - Peter Purves' Flying Circus.

great entertainment, sometimes to his cost.

"I took two weeks to build one layout and I was really proud of it. I thought it was safely stored away in a cupboard ready for that afternoon's show, but then to my horror I saw it blown up by Michael Bentine and his gang from *It's a Square World* for which I made many of the models. I was in tears, not to mention a state of blind panic because there was no way I could rebuild it in time for the show. Bentine was laughing his head off. Then I found out why. It was all a huge practical joke. Bentine's lot had gone to the trouble of building an exact replica of my layout — mine was still downstairs in pristine condition. I could have killed them.

"I remember another particularly complicated layout that I had gone through in great detail with the director at a dress run before we went for a tea break. It was planned down to the last detail — all the points were set and so on. But when we did the show, trains were coming from everywhere except the places I was expecting. It was chaos. I just couldn't understand what had happened. Then I discovered that during the tea break someone had sneaked in from the next studio and had been playing with all the trains. There was a big enquiry. The culprit was revealed to be none other than Richard Dimbleby, who had been thinking about buying a set for his boys David and Jonathan and had nipped in from the *Panorama* studio!"

Of all the *Blue Peter* howlers, two stand out. One was a jolly girl guides' singsong around an artificial camp fire in the studio. Unfortunately, the fire, comprising an electric heater with fake logs, suddenly started to billow smoke and 5' flames leapt in the air before viewers saw three firemen dash in to extinguish the towering inferno.

The other was the immortal *Blue Peter* elephant. Lulu, a young Sri Lankan elephant from

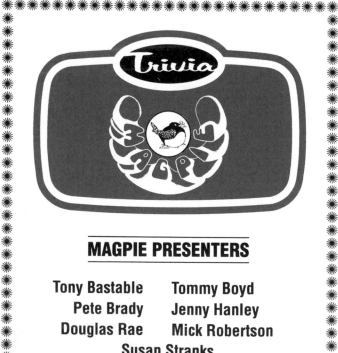

MAGPIE PRESENTERS

Tony Bastable   Tommy Boyd
Pete Brady   Jenny Hanley
Douglas Rae   Mick Robertson
Susan Stranks

Chessington Zoo, came to the studio with her keeper Alec and had already left her deposit on the studio floor before weeing perilously close to Val's foot. This turned the floor into a skating rink and hard though poor Alec tried, he was unable to prevent Lulu from dragging him backwards and forwards across the studio until he eventually slid ignominiously through the lot. Val, John and Peter did their utmost to maintain a stiff upper lip, but as John cheerily said goodbye he stepped back into something soft

Below No wonder the girl is laughing - she's just seen Mick's jumper. Jenny and Doug look the other way.

and black. His parting words were, "Oh dear, I've trodden right in it." A classic moment from a classic show.

From 1968, *Blue Peter*'s arch rival was Thames Television's bi-weekly magazine programme **Magpie**. The aim was to make *Magpie* much trendier than *Blue Peter*, not the most onerous task in the world since the *Blue Peter* presenters gave the impression that they were not terribly *au fait* with current trends. They probably thought Dave Dee, Dozy, Beaky, Mick and Tich were Snow White's new friends.

To this end, *Magpie* recruited three streetwise dudes in Susan Stranks, who as 'a typical teenager' had appeared nine years earlier on the very first edition of *Juke Box Jury*, Tony Bastable and former disc jockey Pete Brady. They in turn were followed by Jenny Hanley, Mick Robertson, Douglas Rae and Tommy Boyd (still going strong today). *Magpie* certainly couldn't be accused of being middle class as *Blue*

Below Magpie *trailblazers - Pete Brady, Susan Stranks and Tony Bastable.*

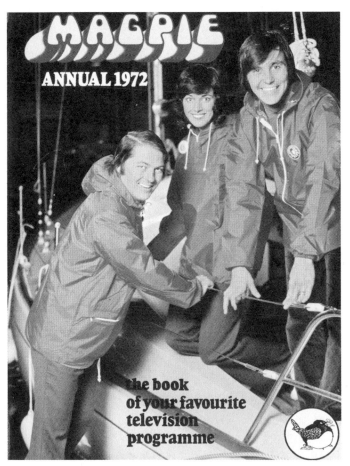

MAGPIE
ANNUAL 1972
the book of your favourite television programme

"Get down, Shep"

Peter had been — *Magpie* featured pop groups as opposed to the Dagenham Girl Pipers — but what the show lacked was a daring exhibitionist like John Noakes. Because they were considerably more fashion conscious, the *Magpie* crowd always seemed happier in the warmth of the studio where they wouldn't get too messy. Whereas good old Johnny thought nothing of courageously canoeing on fast-flowing, white-water rapids, I always felt that the *Magpie* presenters would venture on to the nearby Thames merely to feed the ducks — and then only if it wasn't raining.

One of the first informative series for children was **All Your Own**. Presented from 1954 by the incredibly tall Huw Wheldon, later to become BBC Director of Television, it offered youngsters a platform to show off their particular skills, such as model-making or playing musical instruments. The latter category introduced a youngster who was to become one of our finest classical guitarists, John Williams, and another young guitarist who, interrogated by Wheldon as to his identity, politely gave his name as "James Page." He went on to be Led Zeppelin's Jimmy Page.

One guest who did not enjoy a fruitful or lengthy career in showbusiness was a pet mouse brought along by a schoolboy in company with the lad's other pet, an eagle. While Wheldon was waffling away enthusiastically about how amazing it was that in the wild the mouse would be the eagle's natural prey yet in captivity they were the best of friends, the eagle allowed his natural instincts to get the better of him and suddenly swooped from his studio perch and ate the mouse...

Other early magazine shows were **Playbox**, introduced by Eamonn Andrews with contributions from Tony Hart, Rolf Harris and Cliff Michelmore, and **Studio E**, presented by Vera McKechnie and featuring George Cansdale and his animals. A forerunner to *Blue Peter* was **Focus** in which Percy Thrower gave gardening

Opposite Magpie's *trendy trio - Douglas Rae, Jenny Hanley and Mick 'the perm' Robertson.*
Below Adrian Hill *on* Sketch Club.

tips, Barry Bucknell taught do-it-yourself and Patrick Moore emphasised that he knew his aurora from his borealis. Another distinctive sight was that of Adrian Hill in his smock and beret for **Sketch Club**.

More active pursuits were catered for by ATV's **Seeing Sport**, introduced by Peter Lloyd who signed off each programme with the plea, "And don't forget, look after dear old mum." Regular contributors included Emlyn Jones and table tennis supremo Johnny Leach, while among the schoolboy participants was a young Mick Jagger who was paid £5 for demonstrating his prowess in a kayak. He got plenty of satisfaction.

Tony Hart and Pat Keysall introduced the award-winning **Vision On**, which replaced the unimaginatively titled **For Deaf Children**, and Tony also presented the admirable **Take Hart**. Youngsters in their droves lapped up magazine shows like **Tom Tom** and **How!**. The last named was presented by Fred Dinenage and

Below Pat Keysall and Tony Hart present Vision On.

boasted a regular panel of Bunty James, Jon Miller (who was always explaining how various gadgets worked) and Jack Hargreaves, that wily old doyen of country life. The one problem that was never solved was how to get Fred Dinenage to stop saying "How!".

The seventies brought Chris Kelly and the film series **Clapperboard** (originally scheduled by producer Muriel Young to run for six weeks, it lasted ten years) and Shaw Taylor urging young sleuths to "keep 'em peeled" in **Junior Police 5**. One person who some say should have been arrested years ago is the indefatigable Roy Castle, host of BBC's **Record Breakers**. Although all too often the programme has been designed to accommodate Roy's mercifully

Right Jack Hargreaves caused chaos in the studio when his pipe set fire to his jacket. Don't ask him how.
Below Tom Tom's John Earle (left) and Jeremy Carrad examine the survival kit in an inflatable life raft.

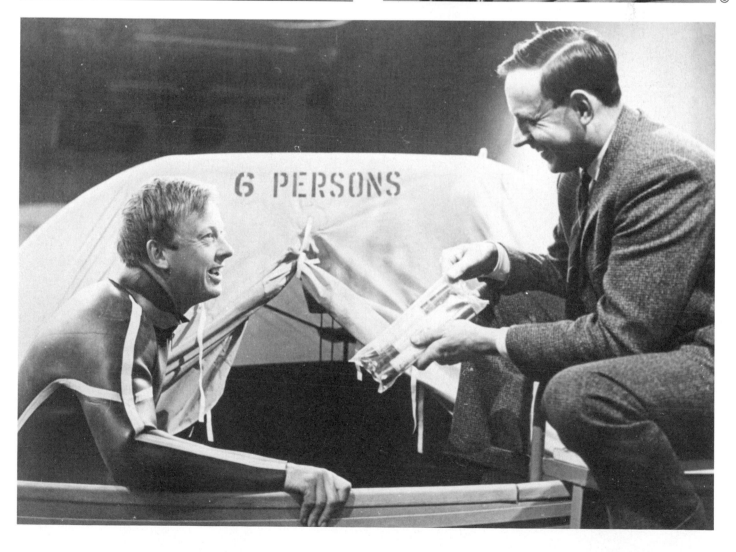

unique talents, his heart is in the right place.

Few programmes have been more informative than **Newsround**, originally known as *John Craven's Newsround*, presented as it was by the man who must have had a team of maiden aunts knitting away feverishly behind the scenes to keep him in sweaters. In fact, he was the first newsreader to be allowed to dress casually without a tie and enjoyed the distinction of having his name above the bulletin. The idea came about after a survey revealed that a mere 0.7% of children watched the news. So the BBC set out to make an easily digestible, Janet and John version with simple explanations of world events and no nasty bits. But over the years it has become more daring and, being ahead of the main bulletin, has even boasted the occasional scoop, such as Mrs Thatcher's elevation to leadership of the Tory Party. After that, nobody could accuse *Newsround* of only bringing good news. ✳

Top opposite "I can play the trumpet," Roy Castle tells a steel band on Record Breakers. "And tap dance. And..."
Bottom opposite The popular How! team: Jon Miller, Bunty James, Fred Dinenage and Jack Hargreaves.
Above left John Craven cheered up when the BBC told him he didn't have to wear a tie.
Above right The talented Tony Hart has been a star of children's television for over thirty years.
Bottom right Before going on holiday with Judith Chalmers, Chris Kelly hosted Clapperboard.

"It's Friday, it's five to five..."

Variety has long been a vital ingredient in children's television. One of the first exponents was **Whirligig**, a Saturday afternoon treat of the early fifties featuring such favourites as Hank the cowboy, his goofy horse Silver King, Big Chief Dirty Face and Mexican Pete the bandit with his beloved Mexican Hat Dance, all the creations of Francis Coudrill. Then there was the obnoxious string puppet Mr Turnip (the invention of Joy Laurey) and his hapless human stooge Humphrey Lestocq, known to all as HL. Lestocq's catchphrases quickly caught on in the playgrounds of Britain, particularly "Goody, goody gumdrops" and "Looky lum." Other *Whirligig* regulars were Steve Race at the piano and magician Geoffrey Robinson, while Rolf Harris made his debut on children's television with Willoughby, a drawing board which sprang to life. *Whirligig* was written by Peter Ling who went on to pen *Crossroads*, thus retaining his association with wooden puppets...

From 1955, if it was Friday and five to five, that meant only one thing: **CRACKERJACK**!

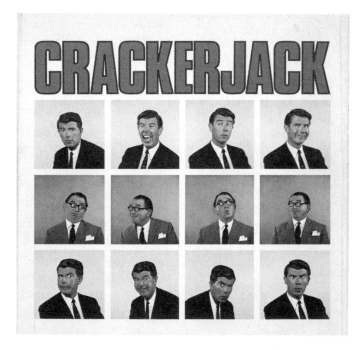

Above Leslie Crowther and Peter Glaze show off their passport photos. *Left* Crackerjack *pair Eamonn Andrews and Ronnie Corbett. Alas, Ronnie won't have grown out of the jacket.*

This was the show with everything — corny jokes, pop star guests, the singalong finale and 'Double or Drop', the game where kids' arms were piled high with prizes if they answered questions correctly or with cabbages if they got them wrong. And it was a disaster if they dropped anything. And of course there were the celebrated *Crackerjack* (repeat, *Crackerjack*) pencils. These humble writing instruments were so coveted that children were prepared to swop their pet hamster for one.

The first presenter was Eamonn Andrews, who I always suspected mimed during the singing. The boxing enthusiast liked children, although he admitted his patience was sorely tested when a seven year-old bopped him in the eye. "It took me all my time not to bop him back," said Eamonn.

Leslie Crowther began his long association with *Crackerjack* (yes, I know, "Crackerjack") in 1960,

Variety shows 71

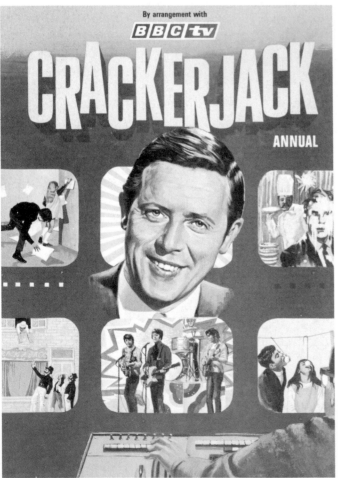

Above Crackerjack. *(From left) Jillian Comber, Michael Aspel, Frances Barlow, Rod McLennan, Peter Glaze.*
Left Crackerjack *(yes, "Crackerjack")* Annual, *Michael Aspel 1970 vintage.*

first as resident comic, then as compère. His partner in crime was the diminutive Peter Glaze (remember him as Tony Hancock's dog in his *Archers* spoof 'The Bowmen'?). Glaze had also been 'spare man' to the Crazy Gang for ten years and had stood in for them all at one time or another. The show also had the royal seal of approval as Leslie Crowther discovered. "After one show we were told that the Queen had been to see us. Apparently she wanted to see *Crackerjack* because her children, Charles and Anne, liked it and she watched it whenever she could. I just couldn't believe that the Queen watched *Crackerjack* and I was still amazed when I met her after the show."

Crowther, who often used to rush straight from *Crackerjack* to do *The Black and White Minstrel Show* (changing in a taxi *en route*), says his own family of five children were fans too. "It was handy having a big family because the children sometimes came up with comedy ideas. One of the great things about *Crackerjack* was that we never played down to the audience just because they were young. We tried to appeal to an audience of all ages. What a lot of people forget is the sheer volume of pop stars of the day who, in the sixties, used to regard *Crackerjack* as second only in terms of exposure to *Top of the Pops*. I introduced countless big names; Roy Orbison, Cliff Richard, Dave Dee, Dozy, Beaky, Mick and Tich. And Tom Jones made his second ever TV appearance on *Crackerjack*."

CRACKERJACK PRESENTERS

Eamonn Andrews	**Leslie Crowther**
Michael Aspel	**Ed Stewart**
	Stu Francis

It was also a good training ground for young comics such as Ronnie Corbett, Jack Douglas, Don MacLean and Rod McLennan, while Michael Aspel and Ed Stewart both learned a lot from their stints as compères. And we mustn't forget the glamorous girls like Pip Hinton, Jillian Comber and Christine Holmes. Pip says: "We all had such fun and even now I still get recognised by ladies in Marks and Spencer."

I hope she fared better than Leslie Crowther, who has this sad confession to make. "I was never given a *Crackerjack* pencil — but I still get asked for them today."

ITV never had anything to compare with *Crackerjack*. The nearest they got was **Little Big Time**, hosted by Freddie Garrity of Freddie and the Dreamers, and **The Five O'Clock Club** with old favourites like Muriel Young,

---

Below *Pinto the kangaroo is happy to hit a man with glasses if it's Freddie Garrity on* Little Big Time.

Wally Whyton, Bert Weedon, Ollie Beak, Fred Barker and Daisy the Cow. The origins of *The Five O'Clock Club* lay in a 1958 show called **Lucky Dip**, set on a children's newspaper and presented first by Neville Whiting and later by Howard Williams. A regular item was 'Happy Cooking' with Fanny and Johnny Cradock. Sometimes their cooking seemed anything but happy as Johnny, a jolly gent in a monocle who always gave the impression that he'd had a drop too much cooking sherry, was bullied around the kitchen by the harridan Fanny. She was the tartar, he was the sauce.

In 1961 *Lucky Dip* became **Tuesday Rendezvous** and two years later the title changed again to *The Five O'Clock Club*. Graham Dangerfield talked about pets, Jimmy Hanley (dad of *Magpie*'s Jenny) made models and Bert Weedon, the man who inspired John Lennon, Paul McCartney and Eric Clapton, encouraged youngsters to take up the guitar.

Weedon recalls: "I happened to say casually on the show that if anyone wanted help with their guitar playing, would they drop me a line. I did not realise then the power of television or the tremendous interest in guitar playing. Three days later Associated-Rediffusion phoned to say there was some mail for me. I said I would pop in and pick it up but they said I'd need a van — there were dozens of sackloads. We had to have thousands of special leaflets

printed. Since then I have been very careful about making off the cuff remarks on television.

"Another time Graham Dangerfield brought a huge eagle into the studio. It was chained to a big log to stop it flying around. When we went for tea break, the bird was left alone in the studio and decided to stretch its wings. It lifted the log and flew over, log and all, to my guitar which was lying on a piano top. When we got back, we managed to get the eagle off but there were great claw marks across my expensive guitar. I've still got the guitar to this day, complete with the scratches where the eagle had landed."

Muriel Young remembers an edition of *The Five O'Clock Club* where an owl was accused of foul language. "Jon Pertwee had been on singing a folk song," says Muriel, "and at the end

Ollie Beak said to Fred Barker that it was nice to hear from that 'old folker'. A woman viewer promptly rang to complain that she had heard a puppet owl swear on TV. It caused a real panic and was relayed back to the director while the show was still on the air. In one ear the poor director was trying to control the show, in the other he was having to listen to accusations that Ollie Beak had used a four-letter word!"

An American visitor to *The Five O'Clock Club* was rotund comedian Stubby Kaye and he moved on to present a sort of mini *Opportunity Knocks* titled **Stubby's Silver Star Show**. This set the pace for further precocious brats to sing everything from 'Hound Dog' to 'The Good Ship Lollipop' on series like **Junior Showtime**, introduced by Bobby Bennett. *Junior Showtime* had a morbid fascination with an outfit called The Poole Family. There were about ten of them to start with and their numbers seemed to increase week by week until they occupied the entire studio. Their 'star' was the youngest member Glyn, who had an extremely minor hit in 1973 with 'Milly Molly Mandy'. The title says it all. However, *Junior Showtime* did manage to unearth one talented act — it was the programme on which singing impressionist Joe Longthorne made his TV debut.

There was no shortage of talent on the inter-school quiz **Top of the Form**, presented by such stalwarts as Geoffrey Wheeler, Paddy Feeny, John Edmunds and David Dimbleby, whose father Richard was once the question master on the radio version. It even spread to a **Transworld Top of the Form** with Bill Salmon in the chair Down Under. Other popular quizzes were the crossword puzzle formula of **Take a Letter**, hosted by Bob Holness now of *Blockbusters* fame, Michael Rodd's **Screen Test** for young film buffs and the noughts and crosses game **Junior Criss Cross Quiz** introduced by, among others, Jeremy Hawk, Chris Kelly,

Top left *Freddie and his spooky Dreamers enter into the spirit of* Little Big Time.
Top right *Bert Weedon about to discover that make-up methods were primitive on* Tuesday Rendezvous.
Left *Little chubby-faced Joe Longthorne doing his bit on* Junior Showtime.

that old Sex Pistols favourite Bill Grundy, Bob Holness, singer Mike Sarne and footballer Danny Blanchflower. Jeremy Hawk was also in charge of the grown-ups show. "Every Wednesday, I used to do *Junior Criss Cross Quiz* in the afternoon and the adult programme in the evening," says Old Harrovian Hawk, former straight man to Benny Hill and Norman Wisdom. "They were intelligent quizzes and the winners thoroughly deserved their prizes. We didn't help them at all — not like nowadays, when on some shows they practically give the contestants the answers."

Story-telling has always been a much loved form of entertainment, even if you side with the theory that the Big Bad Wolf was misunderstood and came from a broken home and that the Three Little Pigs were asking for trouble by not opting for cavity wall insulation. Early pro-

Top Top of the Form - *Geoffrey Wheeler at Hutcheson's Boys Grammar School, Glasgow.*
Above left *Monster maker Ray Harryhausen (left) introduces a friend to Michael Rodd on* Screen Test.
Above right *Jeremy Hawk with two contestants from Granada's* Junior Criss Cross Quiz.
Right *"I'll have a smile please, Bob." Young Bob Holness presents the family quiz* Take a Letter.

ductions, such as Johnny Morris's **The Hot Chestnut Man**, which ran on BBC for eight years from 1953, *Watch With Mother's Picture Book* and ITV's **Once Upon a Time**, were followed in 1965 by the enduring **Jackanory** to which Bernard Cribbins was a regular contributor. And young viewers used to send in their requests and observations to **Ask Aspel**, a series which Michael Aspel claims led to confusion over his Christian name. "I received a number of letters beginning 'Dear Ask...' " ✳

Chapter 6

"We sang Shang-a-Lang"

Above Listen, do you want to know a secret? Billy J. Kramer used to host a Granada pop show, Discotheque.
Left Did girls really fall for The Bay City Rollers? Well, Shang-A-Lang *producer Muriel Young liked them.*

s *Crackerjack,* **Lenny** the Lion and *The Five O'Clock Club* discovered, pop music meant big ratings on children's television. Older kids knew that the weekend started here with Keith Fordyce and Cathy McGowan on **Ready, Steady, Go!,** but a number of shows sprang up to cash in on the craze with younger viewers including **Discotheque,** presented by Billy J. Kramer, **Lift Off with Ayshea,** those tartan teenyboppers The Bay City Rollers on **Shang-A-Lang, Arrows** and **Get It Together** with Roy North and Megg Nicoll. Incidentally, the last four were all produced by Fred Barker's ex, Muriel Young.

GROUPS AND SOLO ARTISTS NAMED AFTER CHILDREN'S TV CHARACTERS

The Magik Roundabout
Casey Jones and the Engineers
Dalek I Love You
Stephen 'Tintin' Duffy
The Flowerpot Men
Gee Mr Tracy
The Railway Children
The Soup Dragons
Spectrum
The Thompson Twins
The Timelords
The Woodentops

There was also Pipkins, but I doubt they were inspired by Hartley Hare, whilst The Stingrays probably took their name from the car.

Roy North has fond memories of the show. "We did ninety-six in all and had all the top names of the seventies on — Slade, Marc Bolan, Gary Glitter, The Bay City Rollers, Mud. We even had some early punk bands on. But bearing in mind it went out late afternoon, Muriel Young would only allow the pretty looking punks to appear. There were none of the rougher ones. And then for the last few years, Ollie Beak and Wally Whyton popped in. What with doing Basil Brush, I couldn't get away from puppets."

I always found it rather disconcerting watching my rock idols reduced to conversing with glove puppets — there was a wonderful example recently on *Going Live*, when to plug her latest album the extremely serious Tanita Tikaram was coerced into attempting some jolly repartee with Gordon the Gopher. It didn't do much for her street cred. But who knows, we may yet see Morrissey discussing the meaning of life with Edd the Duck. ✳

SONGS INSPIRED BY CHILDREN'S TV

Ask Mr Waverly	The Cortinas
Banana Splits	The Dickies
Bat Poem	The Liverpool Scene
Batman in the Launderette	The Shapes
Batman Theme	The Jam
Batman Theme	The Kinks
Batman Theme	The Who
Blue Peter	Mike Oldfield
Captain Scarlet Theme	The Trudy
Charly	The Prodigy
Davy Crockett	Humphrey Ocean
Doctoring the Tardis	The Timelords
Get Down Shep	The Barron Knights
I Trust Valerie Singleton	The Cortinas
Jan and Dean Meet Batman (LP)	
	Jan and Dean
The Lone Ranger	Quantum Jump
Magic Roundabout	Jasper Carrott
Magic Roundabout	The Stiffs
Magic Style (*Magic Roundabout*)	
	The Badman
The Munsters Theme	The Escalators
The Muppet Show Music Hall	The Muppets
Postman Pat	Ken Barrie
Robin Hood	Dick James
Robin Hood	Gary Miller
Rupert	Jackie Lee
Smurf Song	
Father Abraham and The Smurfs	
Star Trekkin'	The Firm
Summer's Magic (*Magic Roundabout*)	
	Mark Summers
Thunderbirds Theme	The Shadows
Tom Baker	Human League
Trumpton Riots	Half Man Half Biscuit
Turtle Power	Partners in Kryme
White Horses	Jacky
The Wombling Song	The Wombles
Worzel's Song	Jon Pertwee

Above Roy North, Meg Nicoll and Ollie Beak Get It Together *on a bike.*
Below Roy North and Meg Nicoll *enter into the festive spirit on* Get It Together.

Chapter 7

"Breaking up is hard to do"

Pop music mixed with drama proved equally popular. By the mid-sixties teenage heartthrobs had advanced beyond David Whitfield and Ronnie Carroll and the success of The Beatles films *A Hard Day's Night* and *Help!* inspired American producers to manufacture a teen appeal pop group of their own to appear in a series of zany adventures. An advert was placed in *Daily Variety* reading: 'MADNESS! Auditions – folk and rock 'n' roll musicians/singers. Running parts for four insane boys, ages seventeen to twenty-one, with the courage to work.' Out of 437 applicants, Peter Tork, Mike Nesmith, Manchester-born Davy Jones (a

Above The boys were originally called The Turtles, then The Inevitables, before finally settling for The Monkees.
Left The Partridge Family, with Susan Dey (top left) and David Cassidy (top right).

MONKEE BUSINESS

Before:
Mickey Dolenz: known as child actor Mickey Braddock, he starred in *Circus Boy* in 1956. Mickey's dad was George Dolenz, who played the *Count of Monte Cristo* on TV.
Davy Jones: jockey and actor, appearing in a 1961 episode of *Coronation Street* as Ena Sharples' grandson Colin Lomax and the first episode of *Z Cars*.
Mike Nesmith: guitarist at Los Angeles coffee houses.
Peter Tork: part-time musician.

After:
Mickey Dolenz: became children's TV producer, responsible for *Luna* (starring a young Patsy Kensit) and *Metal Mickey*.
Davy Jones: went back to the stage and did panto at such venues as the Library Theatre, Luton. Appeared in TV series *A Horse in the House*.
Mike Nesmith: went solo and enjoyed 1977 hit 'Rio'.
Peter Tork: initially formed own band Release before becoming part of regular attempts to revive The Monkees.

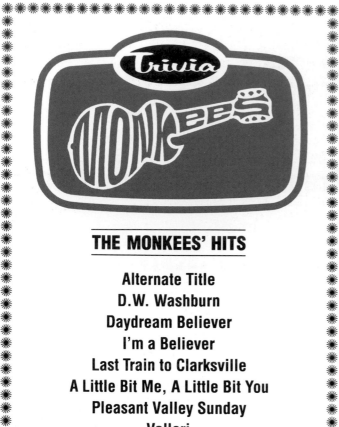

THE MONKEES' HITS

Alternate Title
D.W. Washburn
Daydream Believer
I'm a Believer
Last Train to Clarksville
A Little Bit Me, A Little Bit You
Pleasant Valley Sunday
Valleri

former jockey) and Mickey Dolenz, one time star of *Circus Boy*, were chosen to form **The Monkees**. Monkee business quickly became big business — the comedy was lively and the songs, even though the boys didn't always play on them, were well above average. They were certainly a cut above Herman's Hermits. The quartet were mobbed wherever they went despite some US stations having initial misgivings about screening the show because of The Monkees' long hair. Even after the band broke up, Dolenz made further contributions to children's television as producer of series like *Luna* and *Metal Mickey*.

The Monkees' seventies successor was **The Partridge Family**, a typically bland middle American family with an above average number of teeth. Musical star Shirley Jones played mum, with her real-life stepson David Cassidy as screen son Keith and Susan Dey (now of *LA Law* fame) as daughter Laurie. Cassidy's face

Right *The Monkees - too busy singing to put anybody down.*

Above The BBC axed The Partridge Family *after just one series. Irate fans forced ITV to buy it up instead.*

soon adorned a thousand bedroom walls (at least he didn't need a zimmer like Gary Glitter) and he went on to promote bubblegum, toothpaste and cornflakes. His first hit with The Partridge Family, 'I Think I Love You', sold over 5,000,000 copies, and was followed by a number of group and solo hits. There were also three younger members, including a horrible freckle-faced brat named Danny. They had a mid-Atlantic appeal — and that was precisely where they belonged.

The Brady Bunch (starring Robert Reed, Florence Henderson and Barry Williams) wasn't much better and had considerably less talent than the puppet pop group **The Banana Splits**, starring Fleegle, Bingo, Drooper and Snorky and created by Bill Hanna and Joe Barbera. In between *Arabian Nights* and *The Three Musketeers* cartoons, *The Banana Splits* entertained us with Drooper taking out the trash, a

BANANA SPLITS CATCHPHRASES

"It's time for official Banana Splits club business."
"Hey Drooper, take out the trash."
"What time is it cuckoo?"
"Hey Fleegle, get the mail."
"Ooh, that's a triple ooch."
"And now it's riddle time."
"Uh, oh jango, it's *Danger Island* next."

HANNA-BARBERA **The Banana Splits in HAUL AWAY, JOE**

Authorised edition based on the popular Television Series

A BIG TELEVISION BOOK

Above One banana, two banana, three banana, four...
Right The Brady Bunch, *the epitome of American youth.*

belligerent cuckoo clock, Fleegle unsuccessfully fetching the mail, a talking, flashing moose head, Drooper's trained flea Fletcher, the rival Sour Grapes Gang, Mildred the robot maid and loads of groovy tunes. It actually made it worth getting up on a Saturday morning. ✳

Animal crackers

From the early fifties, George Cansdale had catered for animal lovers in *Looking at Animals* and whilst if we ate all our greens we could stay up and watch David Attenborough in *Zoo Quest* or go *On Safari* with Armand and Michaela Denis, the first wildlife series really aimed at children was **Zoo Time** in 1956. Its presenter was the excellent Desmond Morris who reasoned that because animals were more at home in their living environment, a special television studio should be built inside London Zoo.

Some creatures certainly made themselves at home there. A deadly cobra once slithered out of its basket towards a cameraman who promptly shinned up the camera pedestal and operated the equipment from above. When a vampire bat escaped, bat expert Andrew Watson, wearing a small neck microphone, pursued it across the studio. Halfway across, still in vision, his length of mike cable ran out and he was jolted to a halt by the loop around his neck. Viewers then saw him mysteriously disappear downwards out of sight, seemingly in great pain, accompanied by strangulated noises as he tried to tear off the neck mike. Many watching, knowing nothing about such paraphernalia, were convinced that he had been struck down by the vampire bat and registered their fears to newspapers, who rang up demanding to know whether it was true that a vampire was loose in London and had

already killed an eminent scientist.

Even more embarrassing was the occasion, again on a live edition, when Desmond Morris visited the zoo's lion house. The trouble was the lions decided that the TV camera posed a threat

Above Mistle thrushes, shrews, lions - they were all bread and butter to Johnny Morris. In fact he talked to more animals than Dr Dolittle. It made his show, **Animal Magic**, so popular that he even earned his own cartoon strip in TV Comic.

Left Animal Magic. *Johnny Morris and friend, possibly a pal of* Zoo Time's Congo.

to their masculinity. Morris recalls: "The lion's way of answering this threat was to rush over to his mate and mount her. Since *Zoo Time* was intended for younger viewers, I was at a loss to know how to word my commentary and suggested casually that we might move on to look at some of the other inmates. As we left the copulating pair, with the great male roaring and twitching to a violent climax, a second male came into view. I began to give the viewers some of his personal details — his age, name and weight — when to my audible anguish, he too leapt on his startled female who had been enjoying a quiet snooze in the afternoon sun. Grabbing her by the neck, he too launched into a vigorous mating act, snarling and grimacing in feline ecstasy. I burbled on with an inane commentary about the number of pounds of meat each lion was fed every day while the (no doubt entranced) youth of Britain learned a new meaning for the word 'lionized'. Gratefully, we moved on to the less sexually aggressive tigers and leopards, but in the final enclosure there were more lions and yet another explicit sexual act. This male, however, added something of his own to round off the item. After completing his climactic roar, he strolled over to the front bars of his cage, slowly rotated himself and then urinated with great force straight at the camera..."

Desmond Morris was not the only star of *Zoo Time*. Congo the chimpanzee proved to be such a talented artist that one of his paintings was bought by Picasso!

The other great factual animal series for children was **Animal Magic**, which began in 1962. Johnny Morris had previously had his own radio programme in the West Country on which he did other people's jobs for a day — he sold papers, was a circus hand, etc. It was popular with both children and adults and led first to *The Hot Chestnut Man* and then *Animal Magic*.

"I thought, 'I'll be a zoo keeper at Bristol Zoo,' " says Johnny Morris. "So I got a keeper's uniform and started. And we ran for twenty-one years. I knew a fair bit about animals, having been a farm manager on a 2,000 acre farm, and

my father always used to give our cats voices. Treating animals as humans seemed obvious to me, even though scientists used to decry me for putting words into animals' mouths. It really annoys me when people claim that animals have no emotions.

"The zoo keepers at Bristol were a bit suspicious of us at first but they soon came round, particularly since the programme was good for trade. Usually the animals were as good as gold, providing we adhered to the rules like no sudden movements and no sharp noises. We knew

Right *An attentive chimp gets a picture of his homeland from* Zoo Time *presenter Desmond Morris.*

their levels of tolerance — after a minute and a half they get bored with looking at your face unless you have food. Some assignments were certainly potentially dangerous. I cleaned a crocodile's teeth with a scrubbing brush and went in with gorillas and it was many years before the BBC realised I wasn't insured. In the end, they offered me five times my annual gross if I was killed!

"The episode that sticks in my memory was when we had a young orangutan in the studio. At the end of the show I had him in my arms and was about to say goodbye when he did a filthy great sneeze. Two massive skeins were hanging from his nose so I reached into my pocket for a handkerchief to wipe it. As I did so, he held the pair of them up in a perfect close-up for the camera. All this while the viewers were having their tea!"

Which were the easiest creatures to do voices for? "Camels," muses Johnny Morris. "They always look as if they are talking." And the hardest? "Well, stick insects never seem to have too much personality." ✳

Chapter 9

"Hello, I'm Mr Ed"

Above *Young Jimmy Newton is not convinced by the white horse trying to pass itself off as Fury.*

Instead of merely being supporting acts to cowboys, many horses were promoted to series of their own. The most bizarre was **Mr Ed**, the talking horse. Ed spoke only to his owner, Wilbur Post, who thus received advice on marriage, money and politics literally straight from the horse's mouth. **Champion the Wonder**

Left *Alan Young as Wilbur Post ponders Mr Ed's impression of Esther Rantzen.*

Horse's talents lay in a different direction — rescuing his twelve year-old owner Ricky North (played by Barry Curtis) from all manner of desperate situations, often with the help of Ricky's alsatian Rebel. In real life, Champion was the pride and joy of singing cowboy Gene Autry. Another gallant steed was **Fury**, owned for added pathos by an orphan, Jim Newton. Little

Jimmy was supposed to be the only person who could ride the mighty black stallion, although ironically Bobby Diamond, who played the boy, couldn't ride at all before landing the part. Whatever qualifications he had, they remained well hidden. More sedate equine stars were seen in **My Friend Flicka**, a syrupy story about young Ken McLaughlin (played by Johnny Washbrook) and his best friend Flicka, and, from Britain, **Follyfoot** and the ever popular **The Adventures of Black Beauty**, which starred William Lucas and Judi Bowker as father and daughter.

Anything a horse could do, a dog could do better. There was nothing **Lassie** couldn't turn her paw to — she could open doors, cook a gourmet meal for two and probably assemble an

---

Top right Stacy Dorning took over from Judi Bowker in The Adventures of Black Beauty.
Bottom right Rin Tin Tin knows that by the end of the episode he'll be rescuing Rusty from the foot of a cliff.
Below Steve Hodson and Gillian Blake give Arthur English a tip in the enchanting Follyfoot.

MFI wardrobe in less than the usual three months. By 1960 it was calculated that she had brought 152 villains to justice, rescued seventy-three animals and birds, leapt through forty-seven windows, off thirteen cliffs and on to seventeen moving vehicles — and not all because she loved Milk Tray. She lived in an air-conditioned kennel and was insured for $100,000. On

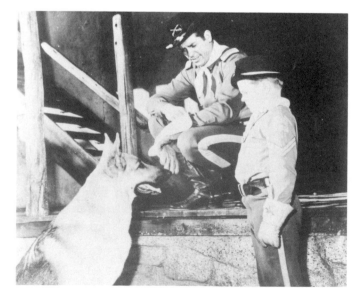

the set she rested on a mobile bed between takes. Her first owner was eleven year-old Jeff Miller, played by Tommy Rettig, who let the side down many years later by being sentenced to five and a half years in prison for smuggling cocaine. You'd have thought Lassie might have sprung him from jail.

Almost as brave as Lassie was **Rin Tin Tin**, the alsatian who joined the cavalry to fight Indians in the old west. He too had a boy master — Rusty (another orphan), played by Lee Aaker.

Underwater stars included **Salty**, the sea-lion, and **Flipper**, the bottle-nosed dolphin who squeaked to fame with Luke Halpin and Tommy Norden as young brothers Sandy and Bud Ricks. Flipper, known originally as Susie, beat off eighty other dolphins to win the part. (I bet there was some backstage bitching over the bucket of herrings that night!) Her trainer said: "To amuse herself, she'll never perform a trick the same way twice. When retrieving a ball,

Above *Bright eyes, sparkling teeth, glossy coat - and Lassie looks good too.*
Below *Flipper, the dolphin, could do more with fish than Fanny Craddock.*

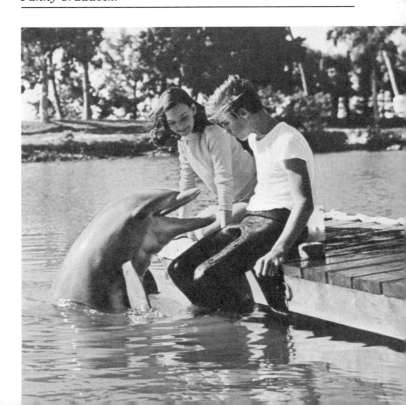

Flipper will first bring it back in her teeth, then balanced on a fin, then on her nose." What a trouper. Even Olivier couldn't balance a ball on his nose.

Dennis Weaver starred alongside big bear **Gentle Ben**, while Australia offered **Woobinda, Animal Doctor**, the tales of a vet in the steamy outback (also known as 'All Creatures Grunt and Smell'), and the legendary **Skippy the Bush Kangaroo**. One of Skippy's co-stars was a young Liza Goddard. It was an experience she will never forget. "I was wee'd on by a wombat and I got lice either from an emu or a koala bear. I had to wash in DDT."

Animals were also an essential part of the fifties show **Circus Boy** starring Mickey Braddock, later better known as Mickey Dolenz of The Monkees. He played Corky, a twelve year-old orphan (didn't any American kids have parents?) adopted by Big Tim Champion's trav-

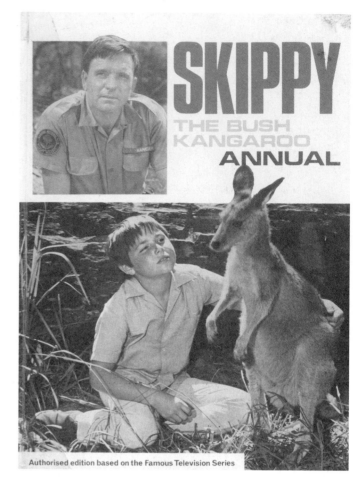

Authorised edition based on the Famous Television Series

Right In 1970 vandals tried to kill the real Skippy in Australia's Watarah National Park.
Below Circus Boy's Mickey Braddock on a lion before he became a Monkee.

Pinky and Perky

Yogi Bear

Above Daktari. *Judy the chimp clearly doesn't think much of Marsh's cooking.*

DAKTARI

elling circus. His constant companions were Bimbo the baby elephant and Joey the clown, played by Noah Beery Jnr some twenty years before *The Rockford Files*. In 1966 came **Daktari**, supposedly set in the Wameru Study Centre in the heart of Africa but actually filmed in a wildlife park south of Los Angeles. It was a bit like shooting *Scott of the Antarctic* on Streatham ice rink. The stars were the animals. Clarence the cross-eyed lion and Judy the chimpanzee comfortably out-acted Dr Marsh Tracy (Marshall Thompson), his daughter Paula (Cheryl Miller) and especially District Officer Hedley (Hedley Mattingly), a stereotyped Briton with bristling moustache and a military bearing. The statutory orphan arrived later in the form of seven year-old Jenny Jones. ✻

Chapter 10

"Who was that masked man?"

Westerns were all the rage in the late fifties when the one question on everyone's lips was: "Who was that masked man?" A fiery horse with the speed of light, a cloud of dust and a hearty "Hi-yo Silver!" meant **The Lone Ranger** was back in action, accompanied by telly's only honest injun. Tonto adhered to the old Indian adage that "white man who speak with forked tongue have heap bad lisp" but he trusted the Lone Ranger implicitly, calling him "kemo sabe" which means 'faithful friend'. After each adventure, the Lone Ranger would ride off into the sunset before anyone could thank him, leaving all around scratching their heads in puzzlement as to his identi-

Left "It's a film crew, kemo sabe," Tonto tells the Lone Ranger.
Right Beneath the mask, the Lone Ranger was Texas Ranger John Reid, sole survivor of an ambush by outlaws.

ty. Clayton Moore played the Lone Ranger with Jay Silverheels as Tonto, and the Lone Ranger was considered such an epitome of American honesty and decency that Moore was later invited to the White House to meet that other pillar of American honesty and decency, President Richard Nixon.

Another bastion of integrity was the man in black, **Hopalong Cassidy.** Hoppy, as he was known affectionately, was played by the ageing William Boyd and had his own Code of Conduct for youngsters, emphasising the virtues of loyalty, honesty, kindliness and ambition. Boyd described Hoppy as "law, order, honour and bravery personified, a cowboy hero with a halo round his head." Hoppy's horse was called Topper.

Duncan Renaldo and Leo Carrillo played that snappy dreser **The Cisco Kid** and his jovial Mexican sidekick Pancho, whose fractured English (phras-

Above Jay Silverheels, who played Tonto, was once a professional lacrosse player in Canada.
Left Duncan Renaldo had played the Cisco Kid in movies since 1945.

Above Clayton Moore made a good living out of The Lone Ranger, *opening supermarkets at £2,500 a time.*

es like "Let's went") was imitated by children on both sides of the Atlantic, no doubt to the dismay of their teachers. But it was all good fun, with each episode ending in raucous laughter and an exchange between the two principals of "Hey Pancho", "Hey Ceesco." If you wondered why Pancho wasn't the fastest mover in the west, it wasn't just his tendency to over-eat. Leo Carrillo was well into his seventies when the films were made. That's why he never chased baddies on a Thursday morning — he was too busy queuing for his pension at the Post Office.

Roy Rogers would burst into song at the drop of his or anyone else's hat. Horses Trigger and Buttercup, dog Bullet, wife Dale Evans and

CELEBRITY STEEDS

The Lone Ranger	Silver
Tonto	Scout
Roy Rogers	Trigger
Dale Evans	Buttermilk
The Cisco Kid	Diablo
Pancho	Loco
The Range Rider	Rawhide
Dick West	Lucky
Hopalong Cassidy	Topper
Gene Autry	Champion

Above "Come in number four." Chingachgook and Hawkeye are upset that their time is up on the boating lake.
Above left Dick West reminds the Range Rider that it's rude to point.
Left Roy Rogers feels a song coming on.
Opposite "It's the cold steel - they don't like it up 'em," says Guy Williams as Zorro.

bumbling Pat Brady listened patiently. Fess Parker was **Davy Crockett**, king of the wild frontier, in a fetching little coonskin cap before going on to play another American frontiersman and folk hero, **Daniel Boone**. Elsewhere, John Hart played **Hawkeye** with Lon Chaney Jnr as Chingachgook, last of the Mohicans; Guy Williams was swashbuckling masked avenger **Zorro**; Alan Hale Jnr played railroad driver **Casey Jones**, whose journeys took him into slightly more dangerous territory than those of Ivor the Engine; and to the refrain of 'Home on the Range', **The Range Rider** (Jock Mahoney) and 'all American boy' Dick West (Dick Jones) rode in unison and spoke in clichés. Hardly a show passed without someone shouting, "Let's get a rope", "This town ain't big enough for both of us" or that old favourite, "We'll head 'em off at the pass." What would they have done if they had been somewhere without a pass? ✳

Chapter 11

"Robin Hood, Robin Hood..."

ntil 1957, television programme planners had left the screens blank between 6pm and 7pm to allow mums to tuck young children into bed and let older ones do their homework without distraction. When the Toddlers' Truce, as it was known, was finally scrapped, ITV hurriedly inserted its new action-packed series like *Robin Hood* and *Sir Lancelot*. Maths homework remained in the satchel until the Sheriff of Nottingham got his comeuppance.

It was never a long wait. For if there was a competition to find the dimmest gang in the history of television, the Sheriff's men would take a lot of beating. Possessing a combined IQ slightly below that of Brain in *Boss Cat*, these warrior wallies made life easy for the Merrie Men by always stopping for a cup of mead or a good chinwag under a tree, thereby enabling Will Scarlett and co to leap down and wound them with sarcasm and the odd club.

Mind you, they were lucky to find a tree because there were only two. The series was filmed on a studio set at Walton-on-Thames with a 20ft high hollow tree trunk on wheels playing most of Sherwood Forest. Because of its mobility, wherever the action went, it followed. It even had its own fake mossy bank. To keep it company, the producers later built another tree out of wood and plaster complete with an over-

hanging branch. Together they made such a lovely couple — it was a pity they had no sap to rise.

The Adventures of Robin Hood was aimed fairly and squarely at the American market (it was Lew Grade's first big moneyspinner). Richard Greene starred as Robin, with Alexander Gauge as Friar Tuck, first Bernadette O'Farrell then *Picture Book*'s Patricia Driscoll as Maid Marian, Archie Duncan as Little John, Paul Eddington as Will Scarlett and

Left Kevin Costner wouldn't have got a look-in with Maid Marian if Richard Greene had still been around.
Right That awful moment when Robin spots that Maid Marian (Patricia Driscoll) has got dandruff.

Alan Wheatley as the poor old Sheriff. In fact, the Sheriff was so detested that Wheatley used to find his car had been deliberately scratched. "I was totally identified with the part," said Wheatley. "Even when I travelled by air, customs officers used to look in my baggage and say, 'Any arrows to declare, Sheriff?'"

Archie Duncan lived up to his heroic role, receiving the Queen's Award for Bravery after rescuing two child actors on the set from the path of a bolting horse. Duncan broke his leg in the process and was replaced for ten episodes by Rufus Cruikshank.

There were guest stars a plenty. Richard

O'Sullivan was one of three actors to play young Prince Arthur (Peter Asher, brother of Jane and later one half of pop duo Peter and Gordon, was another). Other guests included Thora Hird, Leo McKern, Nicholas Parsons, Bill Owen, Wilfrid Brambell and his partner-to-be in *Steptoe and*

Above left No wonder the late Richard Greene retired to Ireland to breed horses after all that activity.
Above right Robin is seized by the Sheriff's men...but never for long.
Below left The Sheriff gives the first known demonstration of fly-jumping while Robin tackles Patrick Cargill.
Below right Young Richard O'Sullivan tells Robin that one day he'll have his own series too.

Son, Harry H. Corbett, who played no fewer than four different roles during the show's 143 episode run. None of these actors had to cope with real chain mail, which was too heavy. Instead, the effect was achieved by spraying garments of knotted string with silver paint.

Even the rousing theme song was a hit, sung by Dick James, backed by the cheers of his nine year-old son Stephen and eleven schoolfriends.

Incidentally, the BBC had earlier come up with their own **Robin Hood** starring Patrick Troughton. There the woodland glades of Sherwood Forest were a handful of trees against a back projection plate of Wimbledon Common (imagine the Sheriff being attacked by The Wombles). On one transmission the background slide was inadvertently put in the wrong way up, so on screen all the trees appeared upside down. Troughton said afterwards: "For one mad moment I considered standing on my head, but realised that this would tax Friar Tuck unduly."

On the next set to Richard Greene's *Robin Hood*, William Russell pranced around as the dashing **Sir Lancelot**. Jane Hylton was Queen Guinevere and Cyril Smith played Merlin (thankfully not *the* Cyril Smith), with Bruce Seton, succeeded by Ronald Leigh-Hunt, as King Arthur. As with *Robin Hood*, the swords were real but the knightly armour was too cumbersome and rubber replicas were used instead. No wonder Lancelot never got the girl — the fair wenches of Camelot probably didn't fancy going out with a fourteenth century Michelin Man.

Meanwhile, over in Switzerland, local lad William Tell was the only man brave

enough to stand up to the outsize Austrian governor Landburgher Gessler. His reward for such defiance was his own TV series.

The Adventures of William Tell starred Conrad Phillips in the title role, with Jennifer Jayne as Mrs Tell, Nigel Greene as Tell's burly pal The Bear and Willoughby Goddard as the evil Gessler. The Landburgher's diet would have reduced Rosemary Conley to tears. He made Henry VIII look anorexic. But because of his liking for the odd whole venison, he lacked Tell's agility and had to entrust his foe's capture to his guards, usually with a loud splutter of "Get Tell!" Unfortunately for Gessler, I suspect his dozy guards were distant cousins of the Sheriff of Nottingham's men.

Conrad Phillips recalls some "hairy moments" during filming. "I was always getting my knuckles slashed in sword fights and once ended up playing Tell from a wheelchair after I broke my ankle in a fall. The crossbow replicas we used were pretty lethal too — they were always shooting off their bolts unexpectedly. But the worst time was when I was sitting on a horse with a rope around my neck tied to a beam and my hands behind my back. They wanted me to have my hands bound with rope, but I had an instinct about the whole thing and just held them behind my back. It was as well

Above *"Now remember, wait for Bernie the Bolt," William Tell advises son Walter.*
Right *After once modelling knitting patterns, Roger Moore posed for chain mail order as Ivanhoe.*

that I did because the horse suddenly galloped away. As it was, I managed to cling to the beam with my free hands, but if they had been tied I would have been hanged."

FROM LITTLE ACORNS…

The following made early appearances on children's TV.

Stephanie Beacham	Rainbow
Michael Caine	William Tell
David Cassidy	The Partridge Family
Ronnie Corbett	Crackerjack
Michael Crawford	Billy Bunter
Judi Dench	Rainbow
Anita Dobson	Play Away
Mickey Braddock (later Dolenz)	Circus Boy
Paul Eddington	Robin Hood
Liza Goddard	Skippy
David Hemmings	Billy Bunter
Jeremy Irons	Play Away
Mick Jagger	Seeing Sport
David Jason	Do Not Adjust Your Set
Patrick McGoohan	Sir Lancelot
Roger Moore	Ivanhoe
Richard O'Sullivan	Robin Hood
Jimmy Page	All Your Own
Prunella Scales	The Secret Garden
John Schlesinger	Ivanhoe
Robert Shaw	The Buccaneers
Dennis Waterman	Just William

One episode featured a young Michael Caine as a prisoner, complete with ball and chain. Any hopes Caine had of an exotic location on *William Tell* were dashed when he found that his scenes were to be shot at a quarry near Watford. And all the mountain scenes were filmed in Snowdonia.

Phillips had been a gunner in the Navy during the War. "So I had a good eye for hitting things. But I didn't fire the bolt which split the apple on the head of Tell's son Walter each week. That was done by trick photography. We used a very fine taut wire through the apple and lined it up with the shot of the bolt speeding towards him. If we had tried it for real, I think we would have got through a lot of boys..."

It was in 1958 that an unknown actor by the name of Roger Moore first burst onto the scene in the tales of Sir Walter Scott's avenging knight **Ivanhoe**, joined by Robert Brown as his trusty sidekick Gurth. Ivanhoe's arch enemy was the same King John who had got short shrift out of Robin Hood. Some people never learn.

Like Conrad Phillips in *William Tell*, Moore performed all his own stunts in the course of which he had his hands slashed, cracked three ribs and was rendered unconscious by a blow on the head from a battleaxe. Moore even managed to injure the series' fencing expert Peter Diamond while filming a fight with broadswords. *Ivanhoe* was an experience which Moore seemed happy to forget. He later remarked: "No one seemed to know what we were doing and we all stumbled about feeling like boy scouts dressed up in armour."

Another future Hollywood star who made his name in an ITV adventure series of the fifties was Robert Shaw, alias reformed pirate Dan Tempest, in **The Buccaneers**. Urged on by a rumbustious seafaring theme song, Tempest swashed a mean buckle, to the constant despair of his rival Lieutenant Beamish (Peter Hammond).

History continued to be a favourite subject for children's dramas in such productions as **Richard the Lionheart** with Dermot Walsh, **Sir Francis Drake** starring Terence Morgan,

---

Above right *"Let's go a-roving," suggests Robert Shaw as* The Buccaneers' *Captain Dan Tempest.*
Far right *Tempest prepares to slice up some more Spaniards off the Caribbean island of New Providence.*
Below right *Would Shaw have looked so invincible if* Jaws *had suddenly appeared over the starboard bow?*
Below *William Russell puts the boot in as Sir Lancelot.*

Dick Turpin with Colin Edwin and **Arthur of the Britons**, where Oliver Tobias took the character back eight centuries in time from *The Adventures of Sir Lancelot* to play Arthur as a sixth century Welsh warlord. Lancelot, Guinevere and Merlin never even got a look in. It can be tough being a legend.

The African bush was the setting for **White Hunter**, featuring Rhodes Reason, and **Jungle Boy**, written by naturalist Michael Carr Hartley and starring his fourteen year-old son Michael Junior as a teenage Tarzan living with a friendly cheetah. Old heroes returned too — Neville Whiting played the intrepid **Biggles** and Laurence Payne was dapper detective **Sexton Blake**. Brian Worth played the dashing detective in **Francis Storm Investigates**, craggy faced Sam Kydd popped up as **Orlando**, a spin-off from the adult smuggling drama *Crane*, while Terence Longdon took the title role in **The Adventures of Gary Halliday**, whose

Above "Shut that door!" Terence Morgan camps it up as Sir Francis Drake.
Right He didn't have the speed or courage of Lassie, but bloodhound Pedro was invaluable to Sexton Blake.
Below Not The Bee Gees, but John Leyton, Neville Whiting and David Drummond in Biggles.

"Robin Hood"

sworn enemy was The Voice.

Created by Charlotte Mitchell, **Kids From 47A** starred Christine McKenna as sixteen year-old Jess Gathercole, Gaynor Hodgson as her fourteen year-old sister Binny and Nigel Greaves and Russell Lewis as her brothers Willy (twelve) and George (nine). Following the death of their widowed mum, the kids, who lived at number 47A in a small block of flats, decided to look after themselves, but faced a constant battle to avoid being split up and put in the care of the local council. However, the one thing they did have going for them was a cunning beyond their years — they certainly had more street cred than the Brady Bunch. Among the show's writers was a young Phil

Left Sam Kydd as Orlando *chases a baddie. Note how Orlando's hat appears to be knitted into his head.*
Right ATV's Kids From 47A *followed the trials and tribulations of the Gathercole family, four children left to run the home without adult help after the death of their widowed mother.*
Below Freewheelers *Mike (Adrian Wright), Jill (Caroline Ellis) and Steve (Leonard Gregory).*

Redmond, *en route* to becoming the mastermind of *Grange Hill* and *Brookside*.

Whenever an evil scientist was threatening to destroy the world, you could be sure that those fearless teenage **Freewheelers** would turn up in the nick of time to thwart their dastardly designs. Produced by Southern Television, this long running drama took our heroes all over Europe on the sort of adventures that youngsters only get up to in TV series. In France they tackled a gang of art thieves who were backed by a deadly secret weapon, they confronted the deranged Professor Nero in a life and death chase through the canals of Amsterdam and in Scandinavia they wrecked a mad Russian's plot to control the world's mineral supplies. And I bet they still managed to get

Above left Jenny Agutter (right) was Bobbie on board the BBC's 1968 production of The Railway Children.
Above right Same characters, different cast. A 1957 adaptation of the ever-popular Railway Children.
Opposite above Sea Hunt's Mike Nelson knows that if the kissing gets serious he'll need that oxygen cylinder.
Opposite below Bernard Hepton as Wemmick and Gary Bond as Pip in the BBC's Dickens classic Great Expectations.

home in time for tea.

Despite all this frantic activity, there was still room for faithful adaptations of such classics as **The Railway Children**. Unfortunately this balmy spring tale was filmed in the depths of winter, which meant that snow had to be scraped away and plastic daffodils planted. The children froze in their summer dresses and the youngest was reduced to tears by the cold. Then there were those wonderful BBC Dickens serials screened at Sunday teatime, which were invaluable if you were studying *Great Expectations* for A-Level English Literature. It was just a pity you couldn't sue the BBC if you failed the exam.

Some of the best drama was imported. Who could forget diving underwater with Lloyd Bridges as Mike Nelson in **Sea Hunt**? Haddock and chips never seemed the same again. Producer Ivan Tors recalled: "We weren't sure at first how much underwater stuff we could get by with but we soon found out that that was what the audience wanted — water, water and more water. The biggest problem was seasick actors. Their faces went green even though we filmed in black and white. We couldn't shoot them — it would have been too ghastly to put on television." On dry land, Ron Ely swung through the trees as **Tarzan**, Paul Birch and William

Campbell starred as tough truckers in **Cannonball**, the mounties always got their man in **Royal Canadian Mounted Police** and in the same country Graydon Gould led **The Forest Rangers**.

The ubiquitous Peter Graves ran Australia's first stagecoach line in **Whiplash**, while in **Whirlybirds** Kenneth Tobey and Craig Hill as daredevil helicopter pilots Chuck Martin and P.T. Moore stumbled across more crime than George Dixon, Joe Friday and Maigret combined. A similar fate befell Ted McKeever and Jim Buckley (played by Larry Pennell and Ken Curtis), the clean-cut parachuting heroes of **Ripcord**. The show's trademark was its skydiving scenes, filming of which could be a hazardous business. Nothing was wasted. When two planes accidentally crashed while shooting an aerial adventure the footage was used later in the series. Down Under, Robert Newton went completely over the top in **The Adventures of Long John Silver**, while Europe produced the enchanting **White Horses** and the extremely silly escapades of master swordsman **The Flashing Blade**. ✳

Above Peter Graves gets cracking in Whiplash.
Left Shiver me timbers, it's Robert Newton as the swaggering Long John Silver.
Below Ripcord's Ted and Jim wonder why they can't get jumpsuits in pretty colours like Anneka Rice.

FROM SMALL SCREEN TO BIG SCREEN

Batman
Daleks: Invasion Earth 2150AD
Dr Who and the Daleks
Dougal and the Blue Cat
(The Magic Roundabout)
The Great Muppet Caper
Head *(The Monkees)*
The Jetsons
The Lone Ranger
The Lone Ranger and the Lost City of Gold
A Man Called Flintstone
Munster Go Home
The Muppet Movie
The Muppets Take Manhattan
Puf'n'stuf
Star Trek: The Motion Picture
Star Trek II: The Wrath of Khan
Star Trek III: The Search for Spock
Star Trek IV: The Voyage Home
Star Trek V: The Final Frontier
Sword of Sherwood Forest
(with Richard Greene)
Teenage Mutant Ninja Turtles 1 & 2
Thunderbirds Are Go
Thunderbird Six
Tons of Trouble *(Mr Pastry)*
Wombling Free
and
a stack of movies involving Lassie and
Rin Tin Tin.

Clarence the Cross-Eyed Lion (Daktari),
Flipper and Voyage to the Bottom of
the Sea preceded the TV series.
Superman and the Mole Men was later
shown as the two-parter
'The Unknown People' on the TV series.

Chapter 12

"Ex-ter-min-ate! Ex-ter-min-ate!"

One of the most important dates in twentieth century history is 22 November 1963, the day President Kennedy was assassinated in Dallas. But the following day is equally significant to television science fiction *aficionados*. For it was on 23 November 1963 that a white-haired old man led two school teachers into a police box and embarked on a succession of adventures through time and space. **Dr Who** had arrived.

The Doctor was the brainchild of Sydney Newman, a Canadian producer who had moved to the BBC from ITV where he had been responsible for the tales of the Wedgwood family in the children's sci-fi series **Target Luna** and **Pathfinders**. For his new project, he envisaged an early Saturday evening series centred around a partly senile 760 year-old alien space traveller who had fled from his own planet to escape from enemy forces. His mode of transport would appear ordinary but was to be much bigger inside than out. Newman also stressed that the show was aimed at chil-

> ### DR WHO – THE DOCTORS
>
> **William Hartnell (1963-6)**
> **Patrick Troughton (1966-9)**
> **Jon Pertwee (1970-4)**
> **Tom Baker (1974-81)**
> **Peter Davison (1982-5)**
> **Colin Baker (1985-6)**
> **Sylvester McCoy (1987-**

dren and that "there should be no bug-eyed monsters."

The opening episode cost a mere £2,500 and began at a normal everyday school where the Doctor's granddaughter Susan Foreman (Carole Ann Ford) was an outstanding pupil. Such was her vast knowledge that science teacher Ian Chesterton (played by former Sir Lancelot William Russell) and history teacher Barbara Wright (Jacqueline Hill) became increasingly fascinated as to her background. They decided to visit her home — a seemingly simple police box which was transformed into a time machine known as the TARDIS. It stood for Time and Relative Dimensions in Space. No sooner had the pair set eyes on Susan's grandfather than they were all whisked back to the Stone Age for a history lesson with a difference.

The late William Hartnell, a veteran of *The Army Game*, played the first Doctor, who he described as "a cross between the Wizard of Oz and Father Christmas." It was when the Doctor encountered a gaggle of performing pepperpots known as the Daleks, with their mechanical cries of "Ex-ter-min-ate! Ex-ter-min-ate!", that the show really took off. Created by Terry

Left It'd be a wow at t'Woolpack, says pre-Emmerdale Frazer Hines. Dr Who (Patrick Troughton) demurs.

Nation, the Daleks made their debut in December 1963. Their flashing lights were the indicator lights off an old Morris car and inside each contraption was an actor sitting on a stool with three castors. Actor John Scott Martin, a regular Dalek, said: "It's like a bubble car on castors and you sit inside and trundle it along with your feet. Inside there's a bit of gadgetry to work to operate the lights, eye-stick and gun. Being a Dalek can be dangerous. Once mine was supposed to blow up but things went wrong and it caught fire. I had to be hauled out quick." Also the actors couldn't remove the tops by themselves, so if the crew forgot they could be left there for ages. One crew member recalled: "We'd never go for a tea break without hearing a muffled cry and it would be some poor perisher who'd been left in his Dalek!"

There was considerable fuss over a press picture taken of some Daleks with their cones off and the actors sitting inside, some puffing away on cigarettes, the feeling being that it spoiled the illusion for children. Nevertheless, the Daleks achieved celebrity status and were

Above William Russell (right) could do with his Sir Lancelot armour as the Daleks move in ominously.
Below Peter Purves earns his Blue Peter badge by helping the Doctor (William Hartnell) and Vicki.

GUESS WHO

The following have all appeared in *Dr Who*:

The late Ronald Allen (*Crossroads*' David Hunter) played Rago the alien in 'The Dominators' (1968).
Gareth Hunt was Arak who, along with his fellow colonists on the planet Metebelis 3, was enslaved by giant spiders in 'Planet of the Spiders' (1974).
John Cleese had a small role as an art critic in 'City of Death' (1979).
Beryl Reid played gun-toting Captain Briggs battling against the Cybermen in 'Earthshock' (1982).
The then unknown Leslie Grantham played Kiston in 'Resurrection of the Daleks' (1984).
Sarah Greene was Varne the Cryon in 'Attack of the Cybermen' (1985).
Jason Connery played rebel leader Jondar in 'Vengeance on Varos' (1985).
Alexei Sayle played a disc jockey on the planet Necros where the Daleks were hatching their latest dastardly plot in 'Revelation of the Daleks' (1985).

---

accorded the honour of a 1964 record, 'I'm Going To Spend My Christmas With a Dalek'. A less menacing villain of the Hartnell years was *Crackerjack*'s own Peter Glaze, who played a Sensorite.

Hartnell quit in 1966, partly because he was suffering from multiple sclerosis and partly as the result of a row with the BBC. He considered that the series had become too evil, particularly with the arrival of the Cybermen, and was unsuitable for children.

His successor for the next three years was Patrick Troughton, the fact that the Doctor had acquired a new head and personality being explained away by his ability to transmute into another human form. Troughton's Doctor was a much jollier character, almost Chaplinesque in his baggy check trousers, and he was joined on his travels by young kilted assistant Jamie, played by a pre-*Emmerdale* Frazer Hines (Annie Sugden wouldn't have let him within miles of the farm kitchen dressed in a sporran). Female companions were scientist's daughter Victoria (Deborah Watling), followed by computer scientist Zoe (Wendy Padbury). "The creatures I disliked most were the Ice Warriors," said Wendy. "They were horrible. They had scaly green make-up and awful hissing voices. They were cold and slimy looking and sent shivers down my spine — even though I knew the actors underneath!"

Jon Pertwee became the third Doctor in 1970. He reckons his all-action Doctor was "a kind of science fiction James Bond" but admitted: "I always loathed the Daleks because I thought they were boring. I wanted my monsters to be down-to-earth. I believe there's nothing more alarming than coming home to find a Yeti in your bathroom."

Pertwee's Doctor also did battle with Autons, Silurians, Sea Devils, Drashigs and renegade Time Lord The Master (Roger Delgado), in the process incurring the wrath of Mary Whitehouse who singled out the episode 'Terror of the Autons' and its killer shop dummies, homicidal plastic daffodils and a deadly doll as being too violent and quite unsuitable for children. The Doctor drove around in his yellow car Bessie and teamed up with The Brigadier (Nicholas Courtney), head of UNIT, and a series of assistants — Liz (Caroline John), Jo (Katy Manning) and journalist Sarah Jane (Elisabeth Sladen).

The last named continued into the Tom Baker era, which began in 1974 and introduced doggie robot K9. With his floppy hat and long trailing scarf (which he often tripped over), Baker was the most flamboyant Dr Who. He was also a committed fan of the show and refuted claims that it was too violent. "The Doctor used to outwit his enemies rather than blow them up," said Baker. "Sometimes we even laughed our villains to destruction." Baker had a healthy rapport with his audience. On his way back from Blackpool one Saturday afternoon he wanted to watch the programme. "I called into a

TV shop. The assistant said she was just closing but kindly said I could go to her nearby house and watch it. When I got there, I found her two kids glued to *Dr Who*. I sat down quietly. Suddenly, one of the children looked across at me, then he looked back at the set, then he looked back at me again. He couldn't believe his eyes!"

Since Tom Baker hung up his scarf in 1981, Peter Davison, Colin Baker and Sylvester McCoy have continued the *Dr Who* tradition. But the programme has steadily declined in popularity and is no longer the force it once was. Maybe Urbankans, Mara and Terileptils seem no more menacing than Earthbound perils like double glazing salesmen, estate agents and the VAT man. Who needs hideous space monsters

DR WHO – ASSISTANTS

The first Doctor:
Susan Foreman (Carole Ann Ford)
Ian Chesterton (William Russell)
Barbara Wright (Jacqueline Hill)
Vicki (Maureen O'Brien)
Steven Taylor (Peter Purves)
Dodo Chaplet (Jackie Lane)
Polly (Anneke Wills)
Ben (Michael Craze)
Jamie (Frazer Hines)

The second Doctor:
Jamie (Frazer Hines)
Victoria Waterfield (Deborah Watling)
Zoe Herriot (Wendy Padbury)

The third Doctor:
Liz Shaw (Caroline John)
Jo Grant (Katy Manning)
Sarah Jane Smith (Elisabeth Sladen)
Brigadier Lethbridge-Stewart
(Nicholas Courtney)

The fourth Doctor:
Sarah Jane Smith (Elisabeth Sladen)
Harry Sullivan (Ian Marter)
Leela (Louise Jameson)
Romana (Mary Tamm/Lalla Ward)
Adric (Matthew Waterhouse)
Nyssa (Sarah Sutton)
K9

The fifth Doctor:
Tegan Jovanka (Janet Fielding)
Nyssa (Sarah Sutton)
Turlough (Mark Strickson)
Adric (Matthew Waterhouse)
Perpugilliam 'Peri' Brown (Nicola Bryant)

The sixth Doctor:
Peri (Nicola Bryant)
Melanie Bush (Bonnie Langford)

The seventh Doctor:
Mel (Bonnie Langford)
Ace (Sophie Aldred)

when you've got Jeremy Beadle? Over the years the Doctor may have fought off Plasmatons, Mummies, Ograms, Gundans, Mechanoids and the odd Voord, but it seems as if the great Time Lord Apathy has finally caught up with him. Maybe it's time to let Zygons be Zygons.

Even amidst the daft frills and flares of the early seventies, **Catweazle** would have been hard pushed to win many awards for sartorial elegance. Dressed in some of Albert Steptoe's cast-offs and sporting a straggly beard, wizened

Above and below *Geoffrey Bayldon as wizened eleventh century wizard Catweazle.*

old Catweazle was totally out of place in 1970, in more ways than one. For he was an eleventh century wizard who inadvertently managed to become trapped in the twentieth century. Naturally he was bemused by it all. He thought the electric light was the sun in a bottle and marvelled at the miracle of the telephone (or "telling bone" as he called it). Heaven knows what he'd have made of Gary Glitter. Created by Richard Carpenter and starring Geoffrey Bayldon, *Catweazle* had two young companions. The first was farmer's son Carrot, the second was the aristocratic Cedric.

Above *The puppet double of Father Stanley Unwin preached gobbledygook in* The Secret Service.

Not surprisingly, the period immediately following man's landing on the Moon brought a surge of interest in science fiction. Gerry and Sylvia Anderson weighed in with **The Secret Service**, combining live action and puppetry and starring Stanley ("deep joy") Unwin; Tarot, mysterious magician hero of **Ace of Wands**, was described as 'a twentieth century Robin

Hood with a pinch of Merlin and a dash of Houdini.' His sometimes sinister adventures featured such fearsome foes as Madame Midnight, Mr Stabs and Mama Doc; **Timeslip** saw young heroes Liz Skinner and Simon Randall travelling in time after falling through

Above *Spencer Banks and Cheryl Burfield starred as Simon and Liz in* Timeslip.

Above *The Tomorrow People were called in to foil a series of Nazi-inspired school riots.*
Right *Even owls have stage secrets. Ozymandias from* Ace of Wands *never let on that his real name was Fred.*

Above Good job the baddies didn't know that The Tomorrow People *bought their guns at Woolworth's.*
Right Crane (David Hedison) doesn't see the joke in Voyage to the Bottom of the Sea.

a 'hole' in a Midlands village; and **The Tomorrow People** were a team of Homo Superiors with telepathic powers operating near an old London Underground tunnel. Among the stars were Nicholas Young and Mike Holoway.

The king of American science fiction was Irwin Allen, who brought us the futuristic adventures of super submarine Seaview, commanded by Admiral Harriman Nelson (Richard Basehart), in **Voyage to the Bottom of the Sea**. The series was a masterpiece of special effects, employing five Seaviews in all, ranging from an 18ft version for surface shots to a 4ft miniature model. Allen's next project was **Lost in Space**, made in 1965 but set in 1997. It followed the trials and tribulations of the Space Family Robinson as they set out to colonise a

VOYAGE TO THE BOTTOM OF THE SEA

David Hedison, who played Commander Crane, once served in the US Navy. "The highest rating I reached was Seaman, 2nd Class. Now I'm Commander. Some promotion!"

distant planet, only for their plans to be scuppered by fiendish enemy agent Colonel Zachary Smith (Jonathan Harris) who sneaked on board and reprogrammed their robot. So they ended up in the middle of nowhere, a bleak, barren place with no sign of life. It was a bit like Mablethorpe in high summer. Then, following a comparatively unsuccessful journey through history in **The Time Tunnel**, Allen came up with the last of his sixties classics, **Land of the Giants**, where the spaceship Spindrift, on a routine 1983 shuttle service, passed through a dense white cloud and emerged in a world in

Above Surely Spock would have been appalled by such habits as blowing bubble gum.

Trivia

STAR TREK

THE STAR TREK CREW

Captain James T. Kirk

Mr Spock

Dr Leonard 'Bones' McCoy

Engineer Montgomery 'Scotty' Scott

Mr Sulu

Lt Uhura

Ensign Pavel Chekov

Nurse Christine Chapel

Yeoman Janice Rand

which everything was twelve times bigger. This made Cyril Smith roughly the size of Africa.

Strictly speaking, **Star Trek** was not a children's show but it caught the imagination of youngsters and adults alike. How many kids wanted to be beamed up from tidying their room to go boldly with Scottie, Bones and co? Fans call themselves 'Trekkies' and over 400 fanclubs still exist, including one purely for grandmothers. Leonard Nimoy, whose big ears became even more popular than Noddy's pal, was amazed to visit an American space station and find that the astronauts wanted his autograph. And William Shatner recalls: "I was sitting in a restaurant in some deserted village in the wilds by the Caspian Sea and this waiter came up. Of course the man didn't speak any English and he was as remote from civilisation as you can get in the world but he said, 'Captain Kirk?' It was bizarre." As Spock would have observed, "Highly illogical, Captain."

We've always loved superheroes and in the

Above Having burst through a wall, Superman George Reeves looks about to burst through his costume.
Below Maybe the instructions will reveal why the Dynamic Duo keep getting oxtail soup when they press tea.

fifties we all looked up in the sky to exclaim: "It's a bird!...It's a plane! It's **Superman**!" George Reeves played the chappie from Krypton and the flying sequences were done by filming him lying on a glass table with the city skyline added later. Tragically, the part typecast Reeves to the point where he was forced to find work outside acting as a wrestler. When he shot himself in 1959, his fiancée revealed that he had taken his life because "he was known as Superman to nine million children but couldn't get a job."

The other great superhero of the Golden Age was the brilliant **Batman**. Ty (Bronco Lane) Hardin was first choice for the part but producer William Dozier eventually cast Adam West along with Burt Ward, an actor who was struggling so much that he and his wife made ends meet by returning pop bottles. Alan Napier played Alfred the butler, even though the actor's first reaction to the news was "What is Batman?", and Madge Blake was introduced as Aunt Harriet to stop Bruce Wayne and Dick

Grayson looking like homosexuals. There were wonderful guest villains (each paid $2,500 a show), including a young(ish) Joan Collins as The Siren. But for me the real stars, apart from the deadpan West, were Neil Hamilton as Commissioner Gordon and Stafford Repp as his clueless colleague Chief O'Hara. You wouldn't put them in charge of a tombola stall at a school fête, let alone an entire police department. No wonder all the world's arch criminals flocked to Gotham City. Over here, the series' effects were not always beneficial. Youngsters started jumping out of windows thinking that Batman could fly and the Caped Crusader himself had to make a special announcement to deter such antics. But most of us survived the 'ZAPs' and the 'POWs' to tune in the next day at the "same bat time, same bat channel." Wholly exhilarating!

A gentler form of sixties TV fantasy came from Germany in **The Singing, Ringing Tree**, part of the BBC's *Tales From Europe*. This offered a stern reminder that the course of true love never runs smooth. Petulant Princess Thousandbeauty had set her hopes on a singing, ringing tree for a wedding present (why couldn't she just have a toaster like everyone else?). The handsome prince who sought her hand, and no doubt in time the rest of her body, searched high and low for such a tree. Finally he found one, only to be turned into a bear by an evil dwarf, hardly the ideal preparation for a spot on *Blind Date*. We hissed at the dwarf and cheered the prince/bear until the couple were eventually united in human form and lived happily ever after. ✳

Right *Christel Bodelstein played the beautiful princess in* The Singing Ringing Tree.

BAT VILLAINS

The Archer	Art Carney
The Black Widow	Tallulah Bankhead
The Bookworm	Roddy McDowall
Catwoman	Julie Newmar/
	Eartha Kitt
The Clock King	Walter Slezak
Colonel Gumm	Roger C. Carmel
Dr Cassandra	Ida Lupino
Egghead	Vincent Price
False-Face	Malachi Throne
Fingers	Liberace
The Joker	Cesar Romero
King Tut	Victor Buono
Lord Ffogg	Rudy Vallee
Louie the Lilac	Milton Berle
Ma Parker	Shelley Winters
The Mad Hatter	David Wayne
Marsha	Carolyn Jones
Minerva	Zsa Zsa Gabor
The Minstrel	Van Johnson
Mr Freeze	George Sanders/
	Otto Preminger/
	Eli Wallach
Nora Clavicle	Barbara Rush
The Penguin	Burgess Meredith
The Puzzler	Maurice Evans
The Riddler	Frank Gorshin/John Astin
Sandman	Michael Rennie
Shame	Cliff Robertson
The Siren	Joan Collins
Zelda the Great	Anne Baxter

Chapter 13

Do not adjust your set

At twenty-nine, married with two children and weighing a modest 11st 12lb, Gerald Campion was an unlikely choice to play Frank Richards' hero of the tuckshop, **Billy Bunter of Greyfriars School**. In fact, casting the famous 'Fat Owl of the Remove' was a weighty problem for producer Joy Harington, who said at the time: "Every fat boy in England came for the part but none was right. Then a friend suggested Gerald Campion. Of course, he isn't fat enough in the tummy — we'll have to arrange that. But he's got the face for it." Besides, Campion had been a devotee of *The Magnet* comic in which the Bunter stories appeared and he was confident he could put on weight. "They called me Fatty at school," he explained in 1952, "but I've since been dieting to keep my weight down. I shan't bother any more. And I love jam tarts — I even make them myself."

Campion adapted so successfully that he made the part his own and over the next ten years the playgrounds of Britain echoed to cries of "Yarooh!", "Beast!", "Blimey!", "Crikey!" and "I say, you fellows." But the use of "Crikey!" landed Bunter in hot water when an Enfield vicar, counting thirteen "Crikeys" in one episode, pointed out that the dictionary defined the word as 'vulgar'. Notwithstanding such disgraceful blasphemy, Bunter proved a favourite with chil-

Left Do Not Adjust Your Set, *it's only David Jason, Michael Palin, Terry Jones and Eric Idle.*
Right A wary Bunter weighs up whether the tiger will fit into a sandwich.

dren and adults alike, to the extent that at one stage his adventures went out live twice every Friday — at 5.25 pm for children and two hours later for their parents. Campion found that public reaction to him had both its good and bad points. "People would send me cakes in the post, but they also used to playfully kick me around if they saw me because that was what always happened to Bunter."

Other than a worldwide doughnut short-age, the great bane of Bunter's life was the form master of the Remove, Mr Quelch, played in the fifties by Kynaston Reeves and in the sixties by Frank Melford. Bunter's chums included Bob Cherry, Harry Wharton and Frank Nugent, the latter played by a young Michael Crawford. David Hemmings and Melvyn Hayes also appeared as boys.

Fittingly, these days Campion is a success-ful restaurateur. It's a long haul from the tuck shop to *haute cuisine*.

Children's television comedy was in its infancy in the early fifties but Richard Hearne was to forward the cause no end with his mad-cap, bowler-hatted creation **Mr Pastry**.

Hearne's mother was a dramatic actress and he made his stage debut in her arms at the tender age of six weeks. He began on TV in the late thirties, but it was not until 1950 that he intro-duced the accident prone Mr Pastry to the strains of 'Pop Goes the Weasel'.

Hearne's best known routine was 'The Lancers', where he charged through a ballroom while dancing with an imaginary partner. His act earned him this accolade from no less a per-

Far left *Slapstick was always just around the corner for Richard Hearne's Mr Pastry.*
Left *Fourteen year-old Dennis Waterman as Richmal Compton's* Just William *in 1962.*
Below *Bonehead hasn't realised that he's supposed to point the gun in the other direction.*

son than Ed Sullivan in 1954: "No British per-former ever has scored the tremendous hit achieved by Richard Hearne on American national television. His 'Lancers' routine was acclaimed by forty million Americans as high art." Hearne was awarded the OBE in 1970 but died that same year after a heart attack.

Other British comedy favourites included little Charlie Drake and 6ft 3in Jack Edwardes as **Mick and Montmorency**, Dennis Waterman as **Just William** and Colin Douglas as slow-thinking crook **Bonehead**, who could barely break into a sweat let alone a bank. Fingers was his equally inept partner and Paul Whitsun-Jones played their harassed boss, a definite Mr Small of the underworld. Boss was forever dreaming up master crimes, although the inevitable failure of his troops to respond led to repeated switches in the course of action from plan A to plan B, and sometimes even plan C, in the course of each episode. Colin Douglas has gone on to appear in many prestigious dramas, but to many he will always be remembered as Bonehead.

Above The Double Deckers *became great favourites on both sides of the Atlantic.*

In 1968, Monty Python was still a year away, but three-fifths of its future line-up, Michael Palin, Terry Jones and Eric Idle, starred with David Jason, Denise Coffey, Neil Innes and the Bonzo Dog Doo-Dah Band in the marvellously manic **Do Not Adjust Your Set**, complete with the immortal Captain Fantastic. This series really was a vital landmark in the creation of Python since it also enabled the team to meet a hitherto relatively unknown cartoonist named Terry Gilliam. And Peter Firth,

Bruce Clark, Brinsley Forde and Melvyn Hayes could be found amongst **The Double Deckers** — a gang of adventurous kids who used an old double decker bus as their clubhouse. They were as unreliable as most bus services.

Family sitcoms from America were often screened over here during 'children's hour'. The best by far was **The Beverly Hillbillies**, the tale of mountain family the Clampetts who struck oil, loaded up the truck and moved to Beverly — Hills that is. The head of the household was Jed (Buddy Ebsen), aided and abetted by his tall, dark and cumbersome nephew Jethro (Max Baer Jnr), shapely daughter Elly May (played by Donna Douglas, who received 100 proposals a week from fans) and crotchety old Granny Moses (Irene Ryan), who still tried

Above The Beverly Hillbillies' *most famous fan was President Nixon. Even so the show ran for nine years.*

Trivia

BEWITCHED

SUPPORTING CHARACTERS

Samantha's husband Darrin Stephens
mum Endora
dad Maurice
daughter Tabitha
son Adam
Uncle Arthur
Aunt Clara
identical cousin Serena
housekeeper Esmerelda
Darrin's boss Larry Tate
Tate's wife Louise
the Stephens' neighbours, Abner and
Gladys Kravitz

Endora called Darrin, amongst others:
Darwin, Darwood, Dumbo and
Dum-Dum

Above and below As if by magic, Samantha had two Darrins, Dick York (below) and Dick Sargent (above).

to buy everyday items like possum innards from the local supermarket. Then there was **Bewitched** starring Elizabeth Montgomery as Samantha, who twitched her nose like Hammy Hamster to bring chaos into the life of her ad-man husband Darrin (Dick York); Larry Hagman in **I Dream of Jeannie**; Fred MacMurray in **My Three Sons**; plus the crazy cop caper **Car 54, Where Are You?**, **No Time for Sergeants**, **My Favourite Martian** and excruciatingly awful proof that God does move in mysterious ways, **The Flying Nun**. Incredibly, *The Flying Nun*, which starred Sally

"Ha, ha!"

THE MUNSTERS

Herman   wife Lily
son Eddie   daughter Marilyn
Grandpa

Their address: 1313 Mockingbird Lane.
Herman's place of work: Gateman, Goodbury
& Graves funeral directors.

Field, was praised by some religious orders for 'humanising' nuns. To my mind, it did for nuns what Christie did for property prices in Rillington Place.

Finally, there was the monstrous double bill of **The Munsters,** featuring Al Lewis as Norman Lamont lookalike Grandpa, and their rivals **The Addams Family,** whose butler Lurch used to inquire: "You rannnnng?" ✳

THE ADDAMS FAMILY

Gomez   wife Morticia
Uncle Fester   son Pugsley
daughter Wednesday   butler Lurch
Grandmama   Cousin Itt
Thing

Gomez's pet: Aristotle the octopus.
Wednesday's pet: Homer the black
widow spider.
Morticia's pet: a man-eating plant called
an African Strangler.

Left The Addams Family's *Morticia (Carolyn Jones) reckons it makes a change from a budgie.*
Top right 6ft 7in Fred Gwynne (alias Herman Munster) *had earlier starred in* Car 54, Where Are You?
Bottom right Kids rarely came twice to play with Pugsley Addams - he kept a gallows and electric chair in his room.

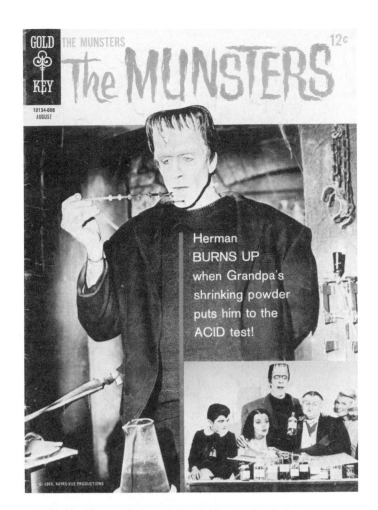

Chapter 14

"Yabba dabba doo!"

Hanna-Barbera produced the best known cartoons during the Golden Age, beginning in 1959 with **Huckleberry Hound**. Old Huck may have been given star billing (to some, his rendition of 'Clementine' alone was worth it), but he was soon overtaken in the popularity stakes by the scourge of Mr Ranger and the Jellystone National Park, **Yogi Bear**. Yogi was definitely smarter than the average bear and his prowess at raiding picnic baskets was much admired by his little pal Boo Boo. The other characters in Huck's show were Mr Jinks the cat, with mouse duo **Pixie and Dixie**. Jinks didn't try to hide his feelings, observing, usually after getting his nose caught in a mouse trap and having his whiskers systematically

Left The Flintstones and the Rubbles pose for a stone-age family snapshot.
Right Huck was the first product of Hanna-Barbera's 'semi-animated' (limited movement) cartoon factory.
Below Bill Hanna and Joe Barbera quickly proved themselves smarter than the average animators.

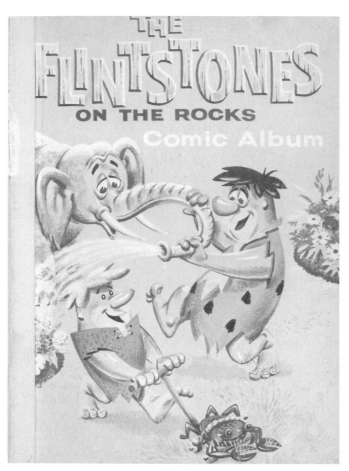

removed one by one: "I hate those meeces to pieces." Further favourites followed — **Quick Draw McGraw** (the law enforcing horse and his Mexican sidekick Baba Looie), **Hokey Wolf**, **Yakky Doodle Duck**, **Augie Doggie and Doggie Daddy**, **Secret Squirrel**, **Atom Ant**, **The Hillybilly Bears** and accident prone lion **Snagglepuss** with his catchphrases "Heavens to Murgatroyd" and "Exit stage left."

In 1960 came **The Flintstones**, the modern Stone Age family who lived at 342 Greasepit Terrace, Bedrock, whilst their neighbours, Barney and Betty Rubble, could be found at 345 Stone Cave Road. Barney's voice was provided by Mel Blanc, the man who put words into the mouths of Bugs Bunny, Daffy Duck, Sylvester and Tweety Pie. The Flinstones had all the up-

Left *Every home should have a mammoth on tap. It meant Fred Flintstone didn't worry about hosepipe bans.*
Above right *That cowardly canine Scooby Doo.*
Below right *Demonic Dick Dastardly in the spin-off series Stop the Pigeon.*
Below *TC hatches another money-making scheme guaranteed to wreck Officer Dibble's hopes of promotion.*

to-date gadgets — a hi-fi on which Fred played 'rock' music (it consisted of a turntable and a bird with a long beak to act as the needle), a vacuum cleaner (a baby mammoth with a long trunk) and a waste disposal unit (a hungry buzzard placed under the sink). They even had a car, which resembled an early Skoda. The family pet was Dino the dinosaur, but eventually they had a daughter Pebbles while the Rubbles adopted a little boy Bamm Bamm.

But arguably Hanna-Barbera's finest hour was **Boss Cat** in 1963. In the States it was known as *Top Cat*, but the title was changed for British consumption because we had a cat food of the same name. TC was the feline equivalent of Sgt Bilko, the idea originating when Bill Hanna heard alley cats making a row near his home. The next day he set about sketching TC, Benny the Ball, Spook, Brain, Fancy, Choo-Choo and the hapless Officer Dibble. The resourceful TC had more fiddles than Nigel Kennedy. I can't help thinking the Americans missed a glorious opportunity by not persuading him to run for

TOP CAT CHARACTERS

Top Cat	Benny the Ball
Brains	Choo-Choo
Spook	Fancy
Officer Dibble	

President.

Also from the Hanna-Barbera stable have come **Wacky Races**, with the devilish Dick Dastardly and Muttley, **Scooby Doo**, the family satire **Wait 'til Your Father Gets Home**, the detective spoof **Hong Kong Phooey** and **The Jetsons**, a kind of futuristic *Flintstones*.

Not to mention from other animation companies **Tom and Jerry** (originally created by

Below Wacky Races *owed its inspiration to the 1965 Jack Lemmon-Tony Curtis movie* The Great Race.

THE WACKY RACERS

Dick Dastardly and Muttley in The Mean Machine
plus
1 **The Slag Brothers in The Bouldermobile**
2 **The Gruesome Twosome in The Creepy Coupe**
3 **Professor Pat Pending in The Convert-A-Car**
4 **Red Max in The Crimson Haybailer**
5 **Penelope Pitstop in The Compact Pussycat**
6 **Sarge and Meekley in The Army Surplus Special**
7 **The Ant Hill Mob in The Roaring Plenty**
8 **Luke and Blubber in The Arkansas Chugga-Bug**
9 **Peter Perfect in The Varoom Roadster**
10 **Rufus Ruffcut and Sawtooth in The Buzz Wagon**

Hanna and Barbera at MGM back in the 1930s), **The Pink Panther** (who began life in the opening credits of the 1963 Peter Sellers film), **The Hair Bear Bunch**, **Woody Woodpecker**, **The Beatles** cartoon, **Charlie Brown**, **The Bullwinkle Show** with Rocky the Flying Squirrel, **Star Trek**, **Astronut**, dim **Deputy Dawg** and his pals Vince the gopher and Musky the muskrat, and, of course, **Popeye**. Incredibly, Popeye and Olive Oyl, the world's first known case of anorexia nervosa, were the same person for a while. When Jack Mercer, who was the voice of Popeye, was unavailable for six cartoons, the sailorman's distinctive tones were provided instead by May Questel, who did Olive! ✳

Top *Why on earth would two grown men, Popeye and Bluto, fight over Olive Oyl?*
Middle *The one and only truly original panther, Pink Panther from head to toes.*
Below *Just a cotton pickin' minute. Deputy Dawg takes a break from guarding the hen house.*

Chapter 15

"Time for bed..."

During the sixties, a number of BBC programmes intended for youngsters acquired cult status with teenagers and adults through being shown at 5.40 in the afternoon, just before the early evening news. After a hard session of double maths there was nothing better than a good laugh at the wobbly sets and wobbly scripts of *Crossroads* (particularly watching Amy Turtle and Mr Lovejoy struggling to remember their lines) and then, before the boring old news, to settle down for a quick burst of something like **The Magic Roundabout**.

Created by Frenchman Serge Danot, *The Magic Roundabout* was first shown in 1965 and owed much of its success in Britain to the dry narration of writer Eric Thompson, father of actress Emma. Another reason for its popularity was its quintessential sixties feel — very laid-back and surreal, to the point that one suspected that Dylan the rabbit could have been on something considerably stronger than lettuce leaves. And Mr Rusty, with his big hat and scraggly beard, definitely looked like an old art school drop-out. Even Florence often wore indecently short skirts. You could see nearly two inches of pipe cleaner!

Other regulars included Dougal the shaggy dog, Ermintrude the cow, Brian the snail, Mr MacHenry, and Zebedee the spring man who would announce his arrival with a 'Boing' and closed each adventure with the familiar "Time for bed." Zebedee was a curious looking fellow, boasting a waxed moustache that would be the envy of Hercule Poirot and bouncing around everywhere on his spring. He must have been a wow in the school high jump. Such peculiarities did not deter his fans however, and a mother in Macclesfield actually called her baby Zebedee.

Left The Magic Roundabout. *Florence gives Dougal a pat - thankfully not one of Ermintrude's.*
Right Like a Rolling Stone - Dylan, The Magic Roundabout's *spaced-out rabbit.*

"Time for bed..."

Above *Arguably the most popular mollusc in TV history - Brian the snail from* The Magic Roundabout.
Left *A great big tuba playing old Hector entertains Za Za and Kiki in Georges Croses'* Hector's House.

The Magic Roundabout became something of a hot potato for the BBC. When it was screened an hour earlier, adults protested that they would miss it and so it returned to the pre-news slot, where it attracted an audience of eight million and was accorded the honour of being named favourite programme by the students of Queen's University, Belfast. When children were asked to make models of the characters, over 100,000 entries were received. And when *The Magic Roundabout* was taken off in the summer of 1968, an army camp petitioned vigorously for its return. Possibly fearing a military takeover of Television Centre, the BBC wisely reinstated Florence, Dougal and co six months later.

The show's successor was another French import, **Hector's House**, known in France as *La Maison de Tu Tu*. It starred Hector (a solemn-looking dog), Za Za the cat and Kiki Frog. Hector used to finish each episode by pouring out his innermost angst and confessing that he was "a great big silly old Hector" or "a great big sad old Hector."

In 1969, Wimbledon Common was taken over by a bunch of Rod Stewart lookalikes called **The Wombles**. Created by Elisabeth Beresford and narrated by Bernard Cribbins, the stories told of the constant struggle of Great Uncle

© Elisabeth Beresford/Filmfair Limited 1991.

Above *The Wombles are still busy keeping Wimbledon Common tidy.*

Bulgaria, Orinoco, Wellington *et al* to keep the Common litter-free. But the lasting memory for many of us was watching these bizarre environment-friendly creatures cavorting around week after week on *Top of the Pops*, since in 1974, in the guise of Mike Batt, The Wombles were the most successful British chart act. It came as a bit of a blow to The Bay City Rollers to be upstaged by the likes of 'The Wombling Song', 'Remember You're a Womble' and 'Wombling Merry Christmas'. Subsequent efforts included 'Wombling White Tie and Tails', 'Super Womble' and 'Let's Womble to the Party Tonight'. Finally they Wombled off, only to resurface in the nineties.

Other occupants of the sacred 5.40 slot included **Babar** the elephant, fearless knight **Sir Prancelot**, **A Bear Called Paddington** (a series based on Michael Bond's famous duffle-coated bear), the Richard Briers narrated **Roobarb and Custard**, **Crystal Tipps and Alistair**, the Ark-ive adventures of nutty **Noah** and niggly **Nellie** and **Herge's Adventures of Tintin**. Poor old Tintin was always in a hurry and from the look of his hairstyle was forever running into the wind. His constant companion was his dog Snowy, while further assistance was provided by old seadog Captain Haddock. And remember identical British secret service agents the Thompson Twins? They even inspired an eighties rock trio to take their name.

Just about the most basic of all animated programmes was **Captain Pugwash**, which began in 1957. Making the characters appear to speak involved the simple process of moving a

Trivia

The WOMBLES

WOMBLES

Great Uncle Bulgaria	Madame Cholet
Orinoco	Tobermory
Wellington	Bungo
Tomsk	Miss Adelaide

© Paddington & Co/Filmfair Limited 1991.

Above Paddington Bear relaxes in his hammock after a surfeit of marmalade.
Right Babar the elephant learns that what goes up must come down - only faster.
Below John Ryan, creator of Captain Pugwash, was also responsible for The Adventures of Sir Prancelot.

Babar characters T17 © 1991. L de Brunhoff.

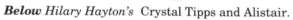

Above *Bone idol, that's Roobarb. But he's always in trouble when Custard the cat is around.*
Below *Hilary Hayton's* Crystal Tipps and Alistair.

Above It looks like the end for Tintin and Snowy. But they'll soon be on their feet again.
Below For all his bravado, Captain Pugwash usually made his excuses and left when the going got tough.

piece of card behind their open mouths. The good Captain was equally simple but fortunately he was regularly rescued from the clutches of his arch foe Cut Throat Jake by the Black Pig's cabin boy Tom. The ubiquitous Peter Hawkins did the voices and the catchy sea shanty signa-

Above Smallfilms' wonderful woolly family the Pingwings started life on ITV.

ture tune has remained a children's favourite, although with character names like Master Bates, John Ryan's stories no longer seem quite so innocent.

Probably the most frequent contributors to the slot were Oliver Postgate and Peter Firmin, the men behind *Pogles' Wood*, *Bagpuss* and **Pingwings**, funny little penguin-like creatures who lived in a barn at Berrydown Farm and waddled around going "pingwing", "pingwing."

Postgate and Firmin's best known film series was probably **Ivor the Engine**, the little Welsh railway engine from the Merioneth and Llantisilly Rail Traction Company Limited. Ivor was fired by Idris the dragon who lived in Ivor's boiler. Peter Firmin says: "The engine driver, Jones the Steam, was based on a Welsh friend of mine, while the stationmaster, Dai Station,

CORRECTION, CAPTAIN PUGWASH

Since this book went to press, we have learned that none of the suggestive names mentioned above and under this notice ever existed in the *Pugwash* series. We apologise to John Ryan, the Captain's creator, artist and author for any distress caused to him by such suggestions. *Pugwash* books and videos are still widely available.

EDITOR

resembled a signalman who used to work on the railways at Harwich and had a rather long, sad, lugubrious face with a drooping moustache." Ivor's great ambition was to sing in the choir like Evans the Song — an idea which came to Oliver Postgate, like all great moments in history, in the bath. Of course, we all knew Ivor was nothing like a real railway — the staff were too polite and the trains ran on time.

After Ivor, the duo dreamed up **Noggin the Nog**, a Viking tale featuring a gentle, affable prince and his evil uncle Nogbad the Bad, who Postgate insists is his alter ego. Students took a particular shine to Nogbad, whose style of ruthless pillaging fitted the image of rebellious youth. Firmin says: "The figure of Noggin was based on the ivory chessmen in the British Museum. I don't know where the word Noggin came from but when I looked it up I found that it meant either a small barrel or a little block of

wood, and I thought that suited a square little person." Other characters were Noggin's Eskimo bride Nooka, the mighty Thor Nogson, Prince Knut, Olaf the Lofty and that weird bird the Graculus.

All of the films were made in the barn of Peter Firmin's eighteenth century farmhouse near Canterbury. He says: "We turned the cow-shed into my studio and Oliver uses the pigsty!" Oliver Postgate admits that it was an exciting if somewhat frightening period in his life. "It was hard going having to make a living by thinking up ideas from a sheet of blank paper, particularly with six children to support. My family had tremendous confidence in my ability to earn enough to feed them — but it was a confidence which I didn't always share..."

Incidentally, years before transferring to the BBC, *Ivor the Engine* started his journey on ITV. Postgate says: "We went out on ITV at 1.15, around lunchtime, which meant that the programme clashed with board meetings at Associated-Rediffusion. But the board members wouldn't dream of missing an episode. They used to interrupt the meeting for a set to be wheeled in, just so that they could watch *Ivor the Engine*. When it was finished, the set was wheeled out again and they carried on with the business of running the company!"

Sadly, these days children's television is not what it was. There are good series about, but financial cutbacks and a certain lack of imagination mean that all too often they are swamped by imported cartoons depicting death and destruction. Fortunately the thriving video industry has enabled today's children to enjoy some of the glories of yesteryear. They may never quite share our suspense as to whether the culprit was Bill or Ben, sing along as vigorously with Pinky and Perky or master the Tracy airwalk from *Thunderbirds*, but at least they will be familiar with the programmes — if only because we'll keep reminding them. For we remember the Golden Age. And we know that the world would have been a poorer place without Spotty Dog. ✳

Below Even the most sinister visitor received a warm welcome from Noggin the Nog.

Above *Bye, bye, everybody!*